Generative AI - From Big Picture, To Idea, To Implementation

SADANAND PUJARI

Published by SADANAND PUJARI, 2024.

Also by SADANAND PUJARI

Master The Psychology Of Weight Loss Via Hypnosis Build Healthy Sleep Habits Learn The Art Of Meditation

Improve People Management And Build Employee Engagement

Content Marketing Masterclass Create Content That Sells

Cyber Security For Normal People Protect Yourself Online

Kanban Fundamentals How To Become Insanely Productive

Positive Psychology Art Therapy: Certified Training

Bookkeeping In Quickbooks Online (Bookkeeping & Accounting)

Business Impact of Digital Transformation Technologies

Learn How to Protect & Restore Yourself from Negative Energy

Generative AI - From Big Picture, To Idea, To Implementation

Table of Contents

Copyright

Generative AI - From Big Picture, To Idea, To Implementation

Copyright © **SADANAND PUJARI**, 2024

Cover design by **SADANAND PUJARI**

First published in 2024 by

SADANAND PUJARI

About

Are you a business leader, manager, or executive? Do you feel confident and ready to embrace the potential of AI and stay ahead of the game in the fast-paced business world?

Our AI 101 online Book is designed exclusively for business leaders and executives like you. In the coming months and years, AI is set to revolutionize the business landscape, presenting both exciting opportunities and potential risks.

Executives, Managers, and Business leaders like you must be able to unlock the power of AI to empower their businesses for the future! But you need to be able to identify the hype from real business opportunities. And risks!

Equip yourself and your team with the knowledge needed to thrive in this AI-driven era. You do NOT need to learn how to code, use machine learning, or deep learning algorithms as a manager!

1. Most AI-related Books teach you HOW to code and use the technical elements of AI.
2. Here you learn the WHY of AI and the BUSINESS IMPLICATIONS of AI.
3. And WHAT you as a manager have to do.

Not only on an AI implementation level. But (even more so) on a human level! Because every AI project will fail if you don't know how to get your people on board! And you will know how to do this after completing this Book.

Discover the Why, Impact, and Plan for AI Adoption in your business. Don't miss this chance to stay ahead in the AI revolution. Our short, professional, and focused chapters allow you to dive into specific areas of interest, tailoring your learning experience to suit your needs.

Unlock the secrets to harnessing AI's full potential for your business success! Secure your place at the forefront of the AI-driven future.

Introduction

Welcome to the program on Artificial intelligence and ChatGPT for executives and senior managers. In the last few years, the awareness and application of AI has increased tremendously. With it, the noise level has also risen. Organizations have even been made to feel that if they don't do something about AI or CHATGPT, now they are going to be left behind. The other dimension in AI is that the core technology itself is changing at a fast pace and many other technologies are also called AI. So it is important for executives and senior managers to understand not just the technology behind AI, but also the broader landscape so you can make smarter decisions.

I'm saying this because one can get confused and lost with all these technologies and jargons that are floating around the landscape. So we will organize different technologies like Cloud, Big Data, RPA industry, 4.0, machine learning, deep learning, NLP, and more importantly, explain how these technologies relate to AI. In addition to this, I'm going to be covering eight real world case studies from different sectors. These will provide clarity on the applications and potential of these technologies. One standout feature of our Book is its continual evolution to stay in step with technological advancements. For instance, we recently added chapter chapters on auto ML, an integral part of AI featuring learning chapters related to auto ML using Google Cloud and other machine learning technical concepts.

Our world and the world of technology took a significant turn in December with the introduction of Chatgpt. So any discussion on AI now involves a discussion on Chatgpt as well. So we have expanded the Book to cover Chat Gpt and the world of prompt engineering. Specifically, I will cover potential starting points for your generative AI initiatives and the challenges associated with data privacy. In essence, our Book is designed to empower you as leaders to navigate the evolving landscape confidently and make informed decisions that drive your organization's growth. I'm Govan and I come with over two decades of experience managing technology, operations and strategy in MNCs and startups, and I will be bringing my experiences and perspectives into this program.

Framework to Assess Organization's Maturity For Artificial Intelligence

In this chapter, I would like to introduce a framework that you can use to assess an organization for its maturity to deploy artificial intelligence and for its maturity to derive value out of the AI deployment. You can do this for your organization or for your client's organization. I have curated these seven factors out of my experiences in deploying AI in my client organizations and in seeing the challenges faced by such organizations firsthand. Let's start with data availability. AI is hungry for data. When I say data, I mean large volumes of data. So data availability is a key requirement. It is not just data, but data at a very granular level and data at multiple levels. Let us say you are in an insurance company trying to detect fraud in motor claims.

You need to know the factors that are driving fraud like age. You need to know the factors that are driving fraud like age, time of accident, a place where the accident occurred, profile of vehicle and data for all these factors should be properly tied to past incidents of fraud. Many organizations may not be ready for this. Some may not be tracking even incidences of fraud, even if the fraud where tracked data for all the factors may not be known or the organization may not even know the comprehensive list of factors that are driving fraud. Even if all the data, 40 factors were available, your linkage of these data to past incidents of fraud may not be there. So if you are not ready with this level of data, you need to first build the pipeline that is the data pipeline.

And you can start an initiative involving artificial intelligence in about a year's time because building the pipeline takes time. That is no shortcut. OK, next is process standardization. If let's say you're trying to automate your invoice process, your process needs to be standardized first before you pursue automation and the process needs to be documented. Also, you may say that you have lots of process documents, but the level of granularity required for automation purposes is vastly different. You need to know which icon in the app needs to be clicked. Is it a single click or a double click or a right click where exactly the invoice document does invoice number appear. Is it in the third line or fourth line from the top or from the bottom?

That is the level of granularity we are talking about here. These things may not be readily available with organizations. Such process activities would even be intuitive to process operators. So there are lots of challenges even in the documenting process to this level of granularity. So assess where you are. That's very important. The number one reason for many RPA that is a robotic process. Automation, deployments to fail is the lack of process standardization and lack of granular level process documentation. The next one is forecast accuracy, do you measure forecast accuracy of your process or your financial process?. What is forecast accuracy ? if let's say you tell your management that you will achieve 10 million this month in your inside sales process, are you achieving 10 million or is it ten point one million or ten point nine million or is it eight point nine million? These things matter for planning because your supply chain can't under plan or over plan because both will have an adverse financial impact.

Forecasting is a process that can be applied in any industry and not necessarily to processes that have a clear financial linkage like the sales process you can try even in a complaint handling or any process in backend operations to in fact, forecasting can be among the first processes for which you can try AI. The key point I would like to make is if your forecasting process is already mature, it makes it that much easier to deploy AI. And every organization would want to have a high forecast accuracy because a higher forecast accuracy would mean that your process is predictable, right? We all want predictability, right. The next one is does your organization have past experiences in managing proof of concept deployments for new technologies, nurturing a new initiative, especially a new tech initiative, involves multiple aspects and challenges like change management.

The process of pitching in for the initiative with your management calculating ROI, getting the sign off with the finance team and tracking that number also all these experiences can be quite helpful when you're introducing a new technology like A.I. Do you have a dedicated staff member to manage the A.I. deployment. That is the next aspect, even if you've outsourced the IT department. the service vendor, it makes sense to have a full time staff member who is knowledgeable in AI for driving the high tech initiative like AI. Also an employee, who is internal to your organization, will be able to navigate the dynamics of your organization better, and you could fix accountability, too, with that dedicated resource. The key here is that the dedicated resource should know enough about AI, otherwise it's not going to help. OK.

Does the organization, especially the top management of the organization? Having a clear idea about what AI is? and how it compares against parallel technologies like RPA, Cloud Internet of Things or IOT and even Industry 4.0 is very important. There is a lot of confusion around these overlapping technologies. And due to rampant overselling, organizations with gullible executives who lack this knowledge are paying a heavy price. Last but not least, is top management ready to support A.I.. Now, maybe the organization has got other priorities and the management team needs attention somewhere else. AI deployment can't be run just by IT alone. IT is only an enabler. You need the support of the entire organization. Evaluate this clearly. So use these seven factors to assess where your organization stands. These are subjective factors, no doubt about it. But they are very helpful to assess where you stand today. You can do this exercise even as a team. I have shared this framework right at the beginning so you can use this framework and the factors in this framework as a reference as you go through the rest of the Book.

Strong AI Vs Weak AI

The interest in artificial intelligence has increased tremendously in recent times due to ChatGPT and generative AI. Generative AI is the technology that fuels ChatGPT. But before understanding generative AI, let us understand what AI is. This understanding is very important and it will help to avoid some fundamental mistakes in the deployment. We are in the midst of change. Not a small change, but a quantum shift. We are in the fourth Industrial Revolution. It is also called Er4 or industry 4.0. Each Industrial revolution brought with it new ways of doing business, new ways of working, and new technology. Industry 4.0 is driven by many technologies and notable among them is machine learning, cloud and advances in sensor technology that has made industrial equipment to interact with one another and transmit their data.

Advances in sensor technology are fueling the industrial Internet of Things or IoT. Other technologies like augmented reality are also important players in industry 4.0. The third Industrial Revolution introduced computers and automation in a big way. The second Industrial Revolution played a pivotal role in the introduction of mass production and many other management concepts. The concept of five day workweek and three shifts in a day with eight hours for each shift, were also introduced during the Second Industrial Revolution. Industry 1.0 is more about mechanization. Now we have generative AI that is fueling the rise of ChatGPT and other applications. I am tempted to say that generative AI is heralding the fifth industrial Revolution.

I hope you appreciate the background I am trying to bring, and it brings us to the fundamental question: what is AI? Keep this question in your mind as we explore another question. We will answer all the questions shortly. Which movie comes to your mind when you think of AI? It could be any of the movies shown here or some other movie. The movies in the top are Hollywood movies, and the ones below are Indian movies. Now a related question is all about what you see in movies. Or is it something else? Well, what you see in movies is actually known as strong AI. Here computers are thinking at the level of human beings. We are not there yet. This type of strong AI is also known as artificial general intelligence and artificial superintelligence.

If you are not at the level of strong AI, where are we today? We are actually at the level of peak I. We call the current state of AI only to distinguish it from the strong AI. It is not really weak. PCA is about solving problems by detecting patterns in data. This is the dominant mode of AI today. A little earlier I used the term pattern. So what is a pattern? We see patterns all around us. We see patterns even in our dresses. You may say that you are wearing a checked shirt and the check is a pattern. So a pattern is something that gets repeated. But what about the frequency of repetition? Should it not be consistent? Yes, it has to be consistent. Is that all too a pattern? I said pattern is something that gets repeated. That something is the characteristic. It could be a pattern in the numbers or images.

So pattern is a consistent recurring characteristic. We use patterns to solve problems in BCCi. BCCi is all about pattern recognition. And pattern recognition is a type of human intelligence. We are bringing that human intelligence into software and hence the name artificial intelligence. We are not bringing other forms of human intelligence like emotion into the software. That is why the current state is called BCCi. Let us now explore the patterns in this visual. What patterns do you see in the visual on your screen? This is a line graph or run chart of sales in a company. Monthly data is plotted for five years starting from 2010 to 2014. So what are the patterns in this visual? Peaks in any calendar year are happening in the month of July. Gloves are. The minimum point in a calendar year is consistently seen in January.

What other patterns are there in this visual? That is an increase and a decrease somewhere in the April -May time frame every year. The increase and subsequent decrease are more pronounced in some years and less pronounced in other years. Are there any other patterns in this visual? There is one left, that is, the peak is increasing at a nearly uniform rate. So merely by looking at the visual, we have identified these four patterns. Can we use this to forecast the future? Absolutely all the patterns we observed earlier or in the future data. So we identified the patterns and we used the patterns to predict the future. This is what happens in AI.

In this scenario, the number of data points is very few. So we were able to do this by visual observation. In real life though, we will use software for pattern recognition and predicting the future. Whenever there is a discussion about AI, there is a mention of the term machine learning. What is this machine learning and how does it relate to AI? While AI is about achieving human intelligence in a system or software, it is machine learning that drives AI. Machine learning is the engine that enables artificial intelligence. So machine learning is the core technology that drives. Deep learning is the more advanced form of machine learning, and deep learning is more suited for analysis involving images, audio, chapter and text data.

ChatGPT uses deep learning. Finally, please remember that machine learning is actually at the intersection of three disciplines: math, programming, and domain knowledge. Why do you think math is important? We learned about patterns earlier. How are patterns represented? Patterns are represented as numbers. Even an image or text is represented as numbers before it is processed by a software program. The third aspect in machine learning is domain knowledge. Your ability to construct an algorithm to identify patterns is influenced by domain knowledge, and domain knowledge plays a very important role in machine learning. A machine learning application developed without adequate domain knowledge results in a low forecast accuracy. That is, the predictions are not accurate or reliable.

Four Types of Data Analytics

In this chapter, I would like to introduce the four types of data analysis approaches. This understanding is very important. Each type has a specific role in the analysis process. Helping businesses to make informed decisions to derive maximum value out of data analysis. We must understand what type of analysis is required for this situation. Is it descriptive or diagnostic or prescriptive or predictive? Each one calls for a different approach. Why is this relevant in the context of machine learning? Descriptive analysis helps you to summarize and understand data. Diagnostic analysis provides insights into why certain patterns exist in data. Predictive analysis forecasts future trends, which is a core goal of many machine learning models.

Prescriptive analysis offers suggestions on how to handle future scenarios, aiding in the decision making process. So machine learning is used widely in diagnostic, prescriptive, and predictive analysis. Opportunity for machine learning in descriptive analysis is really low. In the Descriptive analysis category, we are essentially summarizing what has happened in the context of personal wealth. It is like asking, what was my average weight gain this month in the sales domain? It would translate to querying what was our total sales output last quarter. Moving on to diagnostic analysis. It revolves around understanding why something happened. If you noticed a sudden weight gain last week, you would be trying to find the reasons behind that. Similarly, in sales, if there was a significant surge in sales in the month of, let's say, January, the focus would be on pinpointing what fueled that surge.

Next, we have predictive analysis. Here we are trying to forecast what could potentially happen in the future based on current data. In the health scenario, it would mean projecting your weight six months down the line based on your current habits. In the sales area, it is about leveraging existing trends to predict sales in the upcoming quarter. It is in prediction analysis that we will be using machine learning and deep learning solutions a lot. Lastly, we arrive at prescriptive analysis where we focus on recommending actions you can take to affect desired outcomes in personal health. It is about outlining the lifestyle changes needed to maintain or reduce your weight. For sales, it would imply strategizing to enhance sales performance. In the next quarter.

What Gets Measured Gets Improved

If you want to reduce weight, what could you possibly do apart from exercising or cutting down on calories? What could be the simplest strategy to reduce your weight? Well, what about measuring your weight every day, preferably at the same time of the day? Research has shown that measuring your weight every day would propel you to take actions towards your goal. And the philosophy behind that approach is what gets measured gets improved. This philosophy is pivotal to machine learning or any data analysis. Staying on weight gain example. What do you think could be responsible for being overweight? It could be a variety of factors from eating too much, taking medications like steroids, stress, not having a peaceful and adequate sleep every day, hormonal imbalance, and even genetics.

So all the causes, from stress to medication to sleep are driving the weight gain or overweight scenario. And all these causes are called independent variables in statistics. Weight is dependent on these causes or factors and hence called dependent variables. After all, there is dependency, right? Dependent variable is known by many other names like output variable, reference variable and labeled data. I could express the scenario of dependent and independent variables as an equation y equals f of x, or as y is a function of X1X2X3, x four, x five, and x six. I'm sure many of you would have learnt about this equation in your high school.

This equation is fundamental in machine learning in the agriculture scenario.

If I apply fertilizer regularly, there will be a healthy plantation represented by a growth in the height of the plant. So what would be the dependent and independent variables? In this case, the height of the plant would be the dependent variable because it is dependent on fertilizer. Fertilizer is not dependent on anything else and hence we will call that as an independent variable. If you don't take enough rest or get enough sleep before the exam, you may not be able to concentrate on the exam and hence you may score poorly. You may actually sleep in the exam hall too, as it ever happened to you. So in this scenario, grade is the dependent variable and the number of hours of sleep is the independent variable.

In an automobile scenario, carbon emission of a vehicle is driven by volume of vehicle and weight of vehicle. So carbon emission is dependent on the output variable. In an insurance scenario, charges to be paid by a customer for insuring himself or herself is dependent on many factors like age, body mass index or BMI, sex, smoker status, and so on. An insurance company would demand a higher premium from you. If, in the assessment of the insurance company, you are likely to die sooner. So insurance companies go to great lengths, do a lot of analysis, use machine learning techniques in determining the right cost so that the risk is adequately addressed. This is part of underwriting or risk management by an insurance company.

Why is an understanding of dependent and independent variables important in machine learning? It is important because the kind of dependent variable, the presence or lack of dependent variable in the data set determines the kind of algorithms that we will use. Now look at the two examples on your screen. It is from the insurance industry. The insurance industry can use these factors to determine the insurance premium charges, which is numeric, or use these factors to determine whether an insurance policy should be issued or not, which is a non numeric variable. Both scenarios are possible, and both scenarios can be assessed by using the same set of independent variables. The kind of patterns that will form part of the numeric output will differ from that of a non numeric output.

If the output or dependent variable is numeric, we will use a regression algorithm. And if the output is non numeric like a yes or no scenario, we will use a classification algorithm. In fact, regression and classification algorithms belong to a type of machine learning known as supervised learning. That is, we supervise our. The algorithms to find the patterns relevant to the objective as represented by the dependent or output variable. We understood supervised learning, but what is unsupervised learning? We use unsupervised learning when our dataset lacks a dependent variable. It is quite common in real life to encounter datasets without a dependent variable. Often, organizations don't possess information about the dependent variable linked to various independent factors or variables.

Collecting data for both dependent and independent variables takes a lot of time and effort. Many organizations simply don't have this detailed data readily available. So what is their solution? They begin with unsupervised learning and eventually transition to supervised learning. Generally speaking, supervised learning accuracy is higher that doesn't mean that unsupervised learning is inferior. Unsupervised learning is very effective in detecting clusters and unearthing outliers in data. Outlier detection is very useful in areas like fraud detection.

A different take on the types of algorithms

If you're still not clear of the differences between supervised and unsupervised, or between classification and regression, this chapter will help you. I am inputting three apples for the system to process. All three apples are red in color and they also have a green leaf at the top. The apples are of a particular shape. I am inputting these three images and I am providing a reference for the system to understand that all three images being fed into the system are apples. That reference helps the computer to understand if a similar image is fed into the system in future. System can understand that it is an apple. The system basically looks for the characteristics in an image.

In this case it is the color and shape and also the presence of green leaves. So these three characteristics help to define an apple. Those three characteristics are present. The system will say it is an apple if the characteristics are not present like in this type of apple. The system will say it is not an apple. Look at the way the system is worded. The response. It did not raise an error. It said not an apple. All that the system knows is an apple. Based on certain characteristics we have defined, and everything else is not an apple for the system. In this case, the apple is pink in color and not wine red. Hence it categorizes the pink colored apple as not an apple. If I feed this type of apple, what do you think the system will say? It will still say not an apple, because the protrusion of the green leaf is on the right side, while the apples in our input are on the left side.

Humans can overlook this difference, but systems cannot. So this is supervised learning. That is, we tell the system to learn to identify an object based on certain characteristics. In unsupervised learning, all that the systems can do is group the fruits as apples, oranges, and bananas. Anything other than that is an outlier. So unsupervised learning is very helpful in customer segmentation and also in fraud detection. How do you think unsupervised learning is useful in fraud detection? An outlier is a point of interest in any analysis. An outlier could be fraud. I'm not saying they are frauds, but suspicion is definitely there. Outlier is something that does not fit in with the rest of the data points. Supervised learning algorithms can be divided into regression and classification based on what I am trying to predict. If I am trying to predict a numeric variable like temperature, I will use a regression algorithm. If I am trying to predict whether it is going to be cold or warm, that is a non numeric output. I will use a classification algorithm.

How neural networks operate

In this chapter, let us understand how neural networks operate. Neural networks are part of deep learning, which is considered a more advanced form of machine learning. If you are wondering why I am showing the picture of a shirt, I am going to take the example of buying a shirt. To explain neural networks. Okay. If let's say you are going to buy a shirt. What are the factors you will consider? You will consider one of these five factors. Are all of these five factors right? Would you give equal weightage to these five factors or different weights to these factors? Some of you may give more importance to fit. Someone else may give a higher importance to design.

Someone may give a very high importance to fabric for some other person. Price will be carrying a very high weightage. It all depends on our personal preferences and needs. Right. So how did we arrive at these weights? We have arrived at these weights based on our experiences. As we grew, as we did shopping over years. We know which one of these five factors should carry a higher weightage for a particular scenario. If let's say you are buying a shirt for office purposes, you may give higher weightage to one of these five factors. Right? And when you are buying for leisure wear, something else will have a higher weightage. How are these weights assessed by your mind? It is all based on your experiences, right? So your mind over the Book of time has perfected the art and science of buying a shirt by considering different factors, you know, in your mind.

Right. So the mind considers these factors and decides to buy a particular shirt over many other options that you have. So what is the central concept in buying a shirt? It is about these factors or characteristics and its weightages in a similar fashion. If you are looking at this particular car and if, let's say your eyes are focusing on the bright red color of this car. The red color is processed through your eyes by different neurons in your brain. Your brain has got millions of neurons. Out of those millions of neurons, certain neurons will fire and certain neurons will not fire. And even within those neurons that fire, certain neurons will fire more and certain neurons will fire less.

What you are seeing here is the way neurons process information. You see, some of the neurons are quite active while other neurons are less active. So the color that your eyes focus and the color that is processed by the brain and the color that is synthesized by the brain is all based on the neuron activity. Out of millions of neurons, certain neurons fire. And even within those certain neurons, some neurons fire more. Some neurons fire less. So it is similar to the. Shirt buying scenario where there are certain factors. And within those factors, certain factors have higher weights and certain factors have lower weights. So we bring this concept of neurons firing to process information in the outside world.

So we bring this concept of different factors and different weights that is used by our brains in processing the data so that we can arrive at some prediction. Because machine learning or deep learning is all about prediction. Deep learning mimics the way the human brain works. Just like how we have certain neurons firing and certain neurons not firing. We have some factors for consideration and we leave out factors that are not of importance. Right. Just like how some neurons fire more and some neurons fire less, Certain factors have higher weightage and certain factors have lower weightage. We saw how our brain processes different factors and its importance in buying a shirt. Right. If let's say you choose to buy this car, certain neurons will fire more and certain neurons will fire less and some neurons won't fire at all. That's what happens inside your brain. Okay, So we are going to bring this aspect of the brain. We are going to bring this aspect of neuron firing, neuron firing more and firing less. And some neurons are not firing to process algorithms.

Okay. So the example I'm considering now is a case of the insurance industry. So we are considering these six factors to determine whether someone should be given insurance or not. Right. So I'm taking a simple scenario to explain. We will build on complexity as we go along. Right. So I have these six factors, just like you have five factors in the purchase of a shirt, just like some neurons firing to see the bright red color in the car. Right. I said some neurons fire more, some neurons fire less. Some weights are some factors that are more important in buying a shirt. Some factors are less important. So how does that correspond to these factors? In building a model, we will have weights, right? For the six factors, I have six weights. The six weights can be thought of as relative importance.

Okay, probably more weightage is given for BMI or more weightage is given for whether the individual is a smoker or not. Right. So what is the next step? I consider these factors. I now have the weights. The next step will be for me to multiply the two. Okay, I multiply the two and compute the sum that is factor one into W, one plus factor two into W two. Factor three into W three. Factor four into W four. Factor five into W five. Factor six into W six. So multiplication and computing the sum is my next step. So what do I do next? I use something known as the activation function which we will see in the subsequent chapter to determine the output. I convert this and then I use a function known as activation function to convert the sum into an output.

Okay. What is my next step? I'm still in training, right? I'm learning the process of determining whether an insurance should be given to an individual or not. Insurance policy should be given to an individual or not. So I compare the actual versus predicted. The difference between actual versus predicted is known as accuracy. In mathematical terms, it is known as loss. Okay, we call it a loss function or an error function. Okay. So I compute the accuracy. And if the accuracy is high, it is good. And if the accuracy is not so good, what do you do? You pass the feedback? Back to the wait stage. Right. So I've provided the feedback. If let's say you bought a shirt by giving more importance to, let's say, color, right, the fit is bad. So through your experience, you realize, hey, the fit is not good. I can't use the shirt at all.

So what do you do when you go and buy the next time you give a higher importance to fit and lesser importance to color, relatively speaking. So I adjust the weight. No, adjust the importance. So the same thing I do here also. So this process of giving feedback and minimizing the loss by adjusting the weights based on the loss or error or accuracy is known as back propagation. And the mathematical technique that is used to do this is known as gradient descent. Okay, so this is the process by which I pass the feedback so that I can adjust the weights. I go through this process of adjusting the weights, computing the sum, using activation to determine output and computing the loss. I go through this process multiple times.

In fact, this is an optimization exercise wherein I go through multiple iterations and I arrive at an optimal set of weights that will correspond to a good level of accuracy or an optimal level of accuracy. Right. And then finalized the weights. So once the weights are finalized, the model is ready. I can now take this model and use it for future data to predict. So this is what happens inside a neural network. It is the same way that your brain processes information to buy a shirt. It is the same way your brain processes information when it looks at a particular color. Between a green color and a red color. Certain types of neurons will fire. Certain types of neurons will not fire. Right that corresponds to the factors and that corresponds to the weights. Do you understand now? So this is how neural networks work. This process of iteration, the process of adjusting the weights to arrive at the final set of weights is not visible to us, and hence it is known as the hidden layer. What is known to us is input and output. What happens inside is not known to us. So this is known as a hidden layer.

Understanding Large Language Models (LLMs) and Generative AI

So far we have seen about machine learning, deep learning and neural networks. So where does ChatGPT fit in? That's what we are going to explore in this chapter and the subsequent chapter. There are two terms that are often used while discussing ChatGPT. One is lm r large language models and the other is generative AI. I wanted to explain these two terms as it will help you to understand the technology and the working of ChatGPT. ChatGPT belongs to generative AI. It is a type of artificial intelligence that can generate human-like content. That content could be text images, music and so on. Generative AI is designed to learn patterns in data and then generate new types of content that is similar to the data that it was trained on.

ChatGPT uses a large language model to achieve its objective of generating human-like text. have been trained on vast amounts of text data which forms the foundation to understand and generate human-like text. So what is this large in large language model? Large year refers to the size of the model in terms of parameters. What is a parameter? In simple terms, parameters are the parts of the model that are learned from the training data and they are used to make predictions. ChatGPT has about 175 billion parameters. These parameters enable it to generate remarkably human-like text because they have been trained on a diverse range of text.

But they also mean that the model is very large and requires a lot of computational resources to run. You can think of parameters as something that indicate the relative importance of different characteristics or features involved in making predictions. If you predict whether it will rain tomorrow or not, you will probably consider humidity and temperature. Which one is more important? Depends on the data you have collected. How you indicate this relative importance is known as weights or parameters. A model is nothing but a mathematical representation of real world processes. It is essentially a computer program or an algorithm with multiple steps from input to output. A model refers to the specific system that has been trained to understand and generate human-like text.

This system or model is based on a particular architecture of a neural network. For example, GPT three and GPT four, developed by OpenAI, are based on the transformer architecture, which is particularly suited for processing sequential data like language. During training, the model learns the statistical properties of the language from a large corpus of text data. After training, the model can generate new text that resembles the text it was trained on and it can fill in missing parts of text, translate text, answer questions and perform many other language related tasks. The model actually includes all of the components of the system. The architecture of the network, the parameters that were learned during training and the methods used for training and generating text.

For example, a machine learning model could be trained on a dataset of images of cats and dogs, and it would learn to distinguish between images of cats and dogs on its own. Once the model is trained, it can classify new unseen images as either a cat or a dog. Models can vary in complexity from simple regression models that try to fit a line to a set of data points to large neural networks that can have billions of parameters. We have seen models un large. In large language models. What is this language in the context of large language models? Language refers to human languages like English, French, Spanish, etcetera. These models are trained on vast amounts of text data in one or more languages. The purpose of training these models on text data is to learn the statistical patterns of the language. For example, in the English language, the word often precedes a noun like cat. By learning these kinds of patterns across billions of sentences, the model can generate text that follows the same patterns and therefore looks like natural human language.

Understanding Transformers

In this chapter, we are going to understand the technology behind ChatGPT like transformer technology, neural networks a bit more in detail. Let's start with the very basics. ChatGPT is essentially an artificial intelligence system. Machine learning and deep learning are the technologies that enable artificial intelligence, and deep learning is a more advanced form of machine learning. Both machine learning and deep learning. They learn from past patterns in whatever data we feed into the systems to predict the future. That's how machine learning and deep learning works. Okay. In terms of technology, machine learning is very effective for handling structured data. When I say structured data, I'm referring to data in the form of rows and columns like what you have in Excel files and relational databases.

Deep learning technology is very useful and very effective for handling unstructured data like text documents, emails, social media files, image documents, chapter files, and many more. The dominant mode of artificial intelligence today is known as VI, where we work by detecting patterns and using them to predict the future. The more advanced form of artificial intelligence is known as strong AI. Strong AI is what we see in movies which depict humanlike robotic structures. Strong AI is also known as artificial general intelligence and artificial superintelligence. With ChatGPT. We are touching the outer layer Tof strong AI. Where it's going to take us remains to be seen. ChatGPT uses deep learning.

A basic type of deep learning is known as an artificial neural network. We use the word neural because the way deep learning works is very similar to the way our human brains operate. Okay. In an artificial neural network or any deep learning system, you will have an input layer. A hidden layer and then there is an output layer. Okay. Hidden layer is where all the processing happens. We use the term hidden because the way the processing happens is not accessible to us. A more advanced form of deep learning is known as Convolutional Neural Network. CNN was created to better handle images, chapters and similar types of data. Okay. People are not satisfied, even with CNN. Then we went to a more advanced form of deep learning known as recurrent neural networks or RNN.

RNNs were particularly helpful in NLP. NLP is nothing but natural language processing. It is used in applications like Alexa and Siri. Right. So what is the difference between a simple neural network like a feedforward neural network and a recurrent neural network? In a simple feedforward neural network, information moves in one direction. It moves from input to hidden to output. Whereas in a recurrent neural network, information goes through a cycle of loops. Okay. Here, the neural network is not very good at predicting what is coming next. Okay. RNN is very good at predicting the future. Here only the current input is considered okay, and it doesn't have any notion of order in time. RNNs Consider current input and also the recent past. Okay. Here the feedforward neural networks can't remember what happened in the past except the knowledge from training.

RNNs are able to remember due to their internal memory. It creates output copies of those outputs okay and uses those outputs to loop back into the network. That is how RNNs work, right? People are still not satisfied with RNNs. Hence they went to Transformers. ChatGPT is based on Transformers. Okay. So what is the difference between RNN and Transformers? RNNs were very good for sequence to sequence challenges. Okay. Whereas transformers are good for extended challenges, which obviously means RNNs were not very good when it came to extended sequences. Okay. Because the capacity to preserve information from the initial components was lost, right? So when you have extended sequences, you need to have your system remember all the possible inputs and the associated learning in the transformer.

This past information or past input was not lost. Okay. Transformers use what is known as a self-attention mechanism to weigh the relative importance of different parts in the input. This is a very, very important point when it comes to Transformers. So this allows them to process sequential data effectively. Okay. So the middle layer in the transformer contains an encoder and a decoder. Okay. That's a very important aspect of the transformer model. Okay. The other aspect is that the start of the sentence marker is also fed to the decoder so that the context is better understood. If you ask a question which type of artificial intelligence is better, the encoder decoder model must understand the context in which the different words are said. So that is achieved by the use of start of sentence markers. And sometimes we also use end of sentence markers. Okay.

So to sum up, ChatGPT is essentially a transformer based language model. It uses deep neural architecture, you know, deep learning of artificial intelligence. In fact, it uses a variant of the transformer model, what is called the transformer decoder model. It is designed for language tasks like translation, transcription summarization and also text completion. The important aspect of the transformer decoder model is the Self-attention mechanism. Okay. It gives the relative weights for different parts of data and to process sequential data effectively. Okay. So that is achieved by the Self-attention mechanism. In fact, the transformer model was introduced in a paper titled Attention is All You Need. Okay. And this was authored by Google researcher Vaswani and others.

Is AI an old technology?

What we have seen so far is about the concepts and the technologies behind AI. What we are going to see now is about the technologies driving the rise of AI. If you are wondering what I'm talking about, look at the history of artificial intelligence. It starts from the 50s when Alan Turing, the British mathematician, proposed the Turing Test to assess whether the responses from an AI system is truly human or not. Even today, the Turing Test is the acid test when it comes to assessing the human-like capabilities of AI systems. By the way, who is Alan Turing? He was a very powerful and successful British mathematician who played a very important role in the allied forces led by the British winning the Second World War. He broke the enigma code of the German army.

There is actually a wonderful movie about him on Netflix. Do check it out. Now, coming back to the history of machine learning, it started with Alan Turing proposing the Turing Test in the 50s, and machine learning has developed slowly and steadily since then, and we now have huge interest in AI. Thanks to ChatGPT. So my question is, if AI is such an old technology, what happened in the recent past that is triggering the rise of AI? Don't you think this is an important question? Systems are always hungrier for data. AI systems need lots of data so that it can uncover the patterns easily and effectively. And we need computers that have the ability to process such large volumes of data. So the processing power of computers has improved tremendously over time, and data availability has also improved thanks to the mobile and internet revolution.

The storage of data has also become much easier now thanks to the growth of cloud computing. When these things have improved the cost of data storage, the cost of computing, the cost of mobile, all of them have come down across the board. Just compare the cost of a gaming laptop now with its cost 20 years back. You will know how much you have progressed in terms of processing power and cost. So all these technologies are helping the growth of AI. These technologies, that is big data, cloud computing, are parallel technologies. That is, they exist alongside AI. But those technologies are helping the growth of AI. The other point to note is cloud computing and big data are not AI. They are helping the growth of AI. So let's look at all of this and more in the coming chapters.

Big Data

Big data is part of the evolution of database management. Big Data is about managing unstructured data like chapter files, image files, PDF files and emails. The conventional way of managing such data is not effective. But before seeing big data, let us understand the evolution. Data is stored in databases. Even an Excel file is a type of database. So a database is a collection of interrelated data stored in multiple files. A database management system is essentially a record keeping system. Such a system helps to create, retry, update and manage multiple databases. An organization cannot exist without databases. Databases are needed to avoid redundancy.

We want multiple employees to access, store and process data effectively and easily. We don't want to lose data as well. At the same time, we want to ensure there is adequate protection for data from all areas. All these aspects are achieved with the help of a database management system. Before the modern database management system, we had the file processing system whose main issue was redundancy and inconsistency. Access and handling data is also not an easy process. A modern database management system does not maintain separate copies of the data and they handle the challenges posed by the file processing system rather well.

In relational database management systems, which is the dominant mode of database management in the corporate world today, each table is connected to every other table in the database. Multiple tables are handled effectively using this entity relationship structure. In the student database example that you are seeing on your screen, students and Books tables are connected using a common reference. SQL is a popular programming language for handling and managing data in relational database management systems. We use data definition, language, data control, language and data manipulation language as part of SQL to manage our Dbms. Another important area that is part of the evolution is data warehouse.

In computing, a data warehouse also known as an enterprise Data warehouse is a system used for reporting and data analysis and is considered a core component of business intelligence. Data warehouses are central repositories of integrated data from one or more disparate sources. So big data is characterized by a huge volume of data, which is growing at a rapid pace too. So volume and velocity are key aspects of big data. Huge volume requires huge space as well. If you're wondering what is driving the huge increase in unstructured data, it is essentially the use of smartphones and the growth of social media. Please note that unstructured data cannot be stored in rows and columns, which is the key characteristic of structured data.

Structured data is a relational Database Management system or . RDBMS emerged in the 70s to store data as tables with rows and columns, using structured query language to query and maintain the database. A relational database is basically a collection of tables, which is what we saw earlier, each with a schema that rigidly defines the attributes and types of data that they store, as well as keys that identify specific columns or rows to facilitate access. The RDBMS landscape was once ruled by Oracle and IBM. But today many open source options like MySQL and PostgreSQL are just as popular because of the schema and type constraints.

RPMs are terrible at storing unstructured or semi structured data like chapter files and image files. The rigid schema also makes Rdbmss more expensive to set up, maintain and grow. By the mid 2000, the existing RDBMS could no longer handle the changing needs and exponential growth of few very successful online businesses like Amazon and Google and many non-relational databases were developed as a result of. The challenges and limitations of structure by companies like Amazon, Facebook and Google.

Cloud

When you go to a new city for leisure or for work, you may probably stay in a hotel. You may not buy a house straight away unless your stay is for extended periods of time or when the travel is becoming very frequent to that city. Even if the travel is becoming very frequent, are you going to buy the house immediately? Probably not right. You will stay in a hotel to assess the situation and eventually make a decision whether to buy a house or not. The same thing is playing out in buying equipment used in an enterprise like servers and storage devices. Previously, companies would buy the equipment up front. There was no flexibility and this was a sunk cost. If your needs are reduced, it is actually a loss. Cloud is changing all of that in a big way.

Cloud is about delivery of computing services over the Internet. It is like pay for use and pay as you go. Biggest advantage with cloud is flexibility and you can actually start very small. So this is perfect for startups and small companies. But cloud is increasingly being adopted by large enterprises due to the flexibility and more importantly, the significant cost savings. Cloud relies on sharing computing resources rather than having local servers or personal devices for applications. Software programs are run from servers accessed via the internet and not from servers or computers in your office. Internet based computing where virtual shared servers provide software infrastructure, platform devices. ET cetera.

Are you still not clear about the cloud? Have you used Google Drive or iCloud or Dropbox? They are all cloud services. Previously, we used thumb drives, CDs and floppy disks to store and transport data. Today we use cloud based storage. Even Gmail is a cloud based service. So which is better? Cloud or on prem? Prem is managed locally on a device or devices. It comes with large upfront investment. It suffers from what I would call future locking. That is, the organization can't upgrade the services easily. It also has limited accessibility. All these disadvantages are addressed by cloud services. There are a variety of service models in the cloud for an enterprise to consider.

Another way to categorize cloud deployment is by way of private and public cloud. Remember the example I said in the beginning of the chapter? You could stay in a room that is part of the hotel, or you could take all the rooms in that hotel for rent, thereby ensuring only you and your colleagues stay in that hotel. Or you could even buy that entire hotel. It depends entirely on your needs, your requirements for control, the flexibility you want and the risk appetite you have. I say risk appetite because cloud deployments do come with some security challenges, though they are addressed in a big way by service providers.

The security has improved by leaps and bounds in recent times. One could even go for a combination of private and public cloud infrastructure to manage the challenges that come with public cloud. Do you know that Amazon, as a corporate group, earns more profit from its cloud services than its online business? Such is the power of cloud services and the increasing demand for them. Azure is from Microsoft and Google Cloud followed Suit remains the leader in the cloud market. An area that is related to cloud is about cloud analytics. Cloud analytics is primarily a cloud enabled solution. It allows an organization or individual to perform business analysis or intelligence procedures.

These solutions and services are delivered through cloud models such as posted data, warehouses, SaaS, business intelligence and social media analytics products powered by the cloud. With most businesses moving part of their operations to the cloud. Analytics and BI in the cloud have emerged as the new frontiers of the service model. Today, apps and data are increasingly being deployed to the cloud. The entire process of machine learning is now done in the cloud, thereby saving cost and time. Besides providing much needed flexibility, this has led to cloud analytics and business intelligence, revolutionizing data analysis and reporting in a totally new avatar.

IoT

Iot or Internet of Things is all about connected devices. In Iot, we have a system of interrelated computing devices which may be mechanical or digital machines. They are provided with unique identifiers and they have the ability to transfer data over a network without requiring human to human or human to computer interactions. Iot is everywhere. A car is an Iot device. We can track the car and monitor its performance from our mobile phones and other remote means. Today's airplanes are monitored using Iot systems. Companies monitor the performance of airplanes while they are on air and arrange for appropriate repair when the planes reach the ground. All due to Iot.

Our mobile phone is also an Iot system with multiple Iot systems embedded in it. There are multiple types of sensors in our mobile phone that can do a variety of tasks, like monitoring the heart rate, the number of steps we walk, and even the speed we unlock our phones with the help of a fingerprint sensor. Even a microphone is a sensor. As a matter of fact, it is the oldest sensor in a mobile phone. Measuring oxygen level using an oximeter is also with the help of a sensor. Our homes, too, have become smarter thanks to Iot. We can lock and unlock our homes and rooms, switch on the air conditioners before reaching home, and even adjust the lighting remotely. And this is all due to Iot. Having seen the vast applications of Iot, let us now understand the components of an Iot system. The most important, Of course, is the sensor which collects data from a user or a device and transmits the data to the target.

But more fundamentally, a sensor is a device that measures a signal and processes data from the signal for monitoring, which may even be real time. The Iot revolution is fuelled to a great extent by the evolution of sensors. In its earliest version, sensors were only about measuring and recording a signal. Today, sensors can not just gather data passively, but even interpret it in real time passively. Iot Revolution has meant that there are more interconnected devices on the planet today than there are human beings. All these devices are collecting data about us. The equipment and systems we use and operate.Such data can then be analyzed and monitored by applications to improve our lives and the life of our equipment and systems.

IIoT and Industry 4.0

Today's industrial automation is driven by many technologies like machine learning and augmented reality. And notable among them is the enhancements in the sensor technology. Today we can not only gather data passively and in real time, but we can also analyze and make smart decisions using those data in real time. The technologies of Industry 4.0 are heralding the arrival of truly smart factories. We can monitor the assembly line from a control room and plan for product failures ahead of time. In this photo that you are seeing on your screen, the engineers monitor the performance of the machines and visualize the components in three dimensions using virtual reality. HoloLens, the industry 4.0 technology is also helping to bring down defect rate, manage resources and manage infrastructure better. Well, if the entire factory can be managed remotely, do we really need any lighting in the shop floor? That factory is already a reality.

Industry 4.0 is about optimization, reduced costs, better visibility of processes, supply chain infrastructure and resources. Improved safety is an important aspect. Entire shop floor or the whole factory is today monitored by CCTV cameras. The inputs from CCTV cameras can be processed by advanced machine learning applications to send alarms in real time. If you see automation itself was introduced in industry 3.0, we used it extensively to improve shop floor efficiencies. In industry 3.0, the key difference in industry 4.0 is about utilizing the data from the production flow. In industry 3.0 automation required human intervention. In industry 4.0, we are able to bring down human intervention significantly. While this will definitely bring down costs and improve efficiencies, the reduction in need for manpower is definitely a problem area for the society at large.

An area that is seeing widespread adoption of modern technology is agriculture. The best dates to sow the seeds, how much water to use, and even the ratio in which the nitrogen, phosphorus, potassium, , fertilizers. What should be the ratio in which the fertilizers should be mixed? All these things are today decided by technology, and monitoring is happening remotely and in real time. Asset maintenance is an important benefit of industrial automation. Even if the adoption of automation is low, this is an area worth pursuing. It is entirely possible to bring down the instances of downtime of your equipment in critical equipment. Your downtime is a significant problem area. Some of the issues could be so rare that your manpower is not ready to handle the problem.

When those rare events happen, it is here. That prediction can be a big boon. Predictive maintenance can work alongside your statistical process, control and non-destructive destructive testing approaches. What you are seeing on your screen is actually from a predictive maintenance application that we deployed earlier. The system analyzed the temperature, pressure, age and other details of industrial pumps and predicted the future failure points well ahead of time. You may say that your factory doesn't track granular level data to deploy such applications. You can use the latest advances in sensor technology and cloud applications to first track data and subsequently make use of the collected data. You don't have to spend a lot of money for this. The cost will roughly be equivalent to the cost of just 2 or 3 resources.

Cloud technology allows you to start small and scale up. Once you're convinced. So cost should not be a consideration at all for you to make use of the technology. It is more the willingness. Another concept that is increasingly adopted in product design and asset maintenance is digital twin. A digital twin is a digital representation of an intended or actual real world physical product that serves as the digital counterpart. For practical purposes, such as simulation integration, testing, monitoring and even maintenance. This is used even in the construction industry, since the digital Twin is a visually immersive, accurate and interactive 3D model of a real world space. It allows customers, teams, partners and stakeholders to virtually interact with a physical property. Another interesting area from Industry 4.0 is 3D printing.

The 3D printing process builds a three dimensional object from a computer aided design model, usually by successfully adding material layer by layer, which is why it is also called additive manufacturing. These are early days as far as digital twins and 3D printing are concerned. As days go by, the adoption of 3D printing and digital twins is expected to increase significantly. 3D printing can be used to create equipment to create spare parts and many other application areas, not just in the industrial space, but even in health care.

A quick summary

I would like to summarize a few concepts related to machine learning in this chapter. There are two broad types of machine learning, namely supervised and unsupervised machine learning. If reference or label is there, it is known as supervised. If the label is not there, it is known as unsupervised learning. This label is also known as a dependent variable In the world of statistics, machine learning works by understanding the pattern. So this reference acts as a guiding light to the algorithm, and the algorithm is able to direct its efforts towards finding those patterns relevant to the label. So this label data, the presence of the absence of it is very important in machine learning. Here, supervised algorithms can be further divided into regression and classification. Regression is used when we have to predict numeric values.

When we have non numeric data, we use a classification algorithm. When I say non-numeric, I'm referring to yes or no. Go or no go or grade A, B or C kind of scenarios. We use unsupervised learning to identify clusters and outliers. Remember, unsupervised learning does not have a label or reference. Cluster is like customer segmentation. An outlier is something that doesn't fit with the rest of the data. Outlier is a huge opportunity area used extensively in the world of surveillance and fraud detection. Now, let me give you an example so that you understand the different types of machine learning. A company could use customer information like annual income spending score and other details to determine how much the customer will spend on luxury products.

If the prediction is about the quantum of spend that is numeric, we will use regression. On the other hand, if you are trying to determine whether the customer will buy a luxury product or not, we are talking of a yes or no scenario. That will be classification. The x one to x five and Y mentioned here correspond to independent and dependent variables respectively. The dependent variable or Y is also known as the output variable or reference variable or the labeled data. If this reference or label or output variable is not there in the data set, the algorithm will use the customer information to identify customer segments and any outliers that will be unsupervised machine learning.

Case Study 1: Insurance Fraud Detection

In this chapter, we will see how machine learning is used in fraud detection. I picked up fraud because fraud is everywhere and fraud is a fascinating area in many ways. Fraud happens in all types of companies MNC, mid-sized companies, and even startups. And fraud happens in both high income as well as low income countries. Fraudsters are always smarter, and they adopt innovative ways to commit fraud. That is why catching fraud is not easy. Also, once a fraud has been committed, the onus of proving fraud is on the person or the organization on whom the fraud has been committed, and it is not on the fraudster. So prevention is very important in fraud, and machine learning can help immensely. We will see the application of machine learning in predicting fraud in the insurance sector.

The insurance industry is notorious for fraud. The extent of fraud could vary anywhere from 5% to 15%, depending on the geography and the nature of insurance. Prior to the implementation of the Machine learning solution, this general insurance company used a variety of traditional approaches to detect fraud, like picking a random claim for audit, checking claims beyond a certain threshold limit and auditing new customers. I have seen that some insurance companies adopt an aggregate score method where a risk score is computed for every claim. This risk score is a weighted average of multiple parameters and claims above a certain threshold. Value is passed on to the fraud audit team.

Predictability is low in this effort. The general insurance company has identified motor claims to be the area to deploy machine learning. First, we kick start the Machine learning program by identifying the factors that will contribute to fraud. In this scenario, the team has identified more than 20 factors across customer info, claim info, vehicle info and processing info. This is fairly comprehensive and the team has spent nearly three months pulling this data from multiple sources. Remember the quality and the quantity of the data play a critical role in ensuring a high forecast accuracy for the model. We are predicting with the help of machine learning here.

So accuracy is very important and prediction is happening in a sensitive area like fraud. When I say model, I am referring to the machine learning solution. Model is nothing but a mathematical equation that will be developed and used to predict fraud. The mathematical equation will correspond to the patterns relevant for prediction. The factors are nothing but the independent variables or the X's. Now, the past instances of fraud are needed to direct the algorithm. The algorithm will identify patterns, but what type of patterns the algorithm will find depends on the dependent variable or y. That is nothing but past instances of fraud. Remember, we are trying to predict whether a particular motor claim is fraudulent or not.

So we will use a classification algorithm like logistic regression or decision tree. Now the machine learning algorithm will develop a mathematical equation using which we can predict whether the claim is fraudulent or not. In the world of fraud detection, we use the term potentially fraudulent. We don't say fraudulent or fraud because that is a statement with certainty. Now, I would like to introduce a variation to the scenario we just saw. What if the past instances of fraud are not available? Can you make use of the same algorithm? Well, you can't use the same algorithm because that algorithm requires past references to fraud.

This kind of scenario where past references to fraud or the dependent variable information not being available happens even with large and metrics driven companies. You may have a tracking for fraudulent claims. You may even track the percentage of fraudulent claims. What I am talking about here is a data of past history of claims that can be tied back to these parameters. This calls for a lot of dedicated effort. So many companies won't have this kind of data readily available. What will you do in such a scenario? Will you forget about machine learning? There is a wonderful area in machine learning known as anomaly detection. Anomaly detection is a type of unsupervised learning where label data are dependent. Variable information is not required. An anomaly is something that doesn't fit with the rest of the data points.

An anomaly is not just an outlier. Please remember that as you can see in the graphical plot, a point that corresponds to the change in direction is also an anomaly point in the context of fraud detection. Anomaly detection is a wonderful algorithm, especially in scenarios where labeled data is not available. So organizations who don't have ready made, labeled data available could start off with unsupervised learning. Build a data set of labeled data and then move to supervised learning.

Evaluating the accuracy of machine learning models

An important aspect of machine learning is how to assess the accuracy of the algorithms. Machine learning is all about predictability and any prediction has to be assessed for its accuracy. We use a number of metrics to evaluate accuracy, and the simplest of them is accuracy itself. That is how many were predicted accurately as a percentage of total. In machine learning, we expand this assessment as true. Positive. True. Negative. False. Positive and false. Negative. False Positive is also known as type one error and false negative is known as type two error. So accuracy is true. Positive plus true. Negative divided by a total of all the possible scenarios. Now let us consider the fraud detection scenario with some numbers so you understand the concept of true positive, true.

Negative. False. Positive and false negative. I've summarized the outcome of the prediction in the form of a table. This table is also known as confusion matrix. Number of fraudulent transactions correctly classified by the model or true positive is 80% of legitimate transactions. Correctly classified by the model is true negative. Both are good scenarios. Now the number of fraudulent transactions incorrectly classified as legitimate is 20. This is false positive and the number of legitimate transactions incorrectly flagged as fraud or false negative is ten. So the accuracy will be 97% out of 1000 transactions. The model correctly identified 970 of them either as fraud or legitimate. This seems impressive, but remember, accuracy can be misleading at times. So let us look at other metrics.

We will start with precision. We have a precision score of 80%. What does this mean? Precision answers an important question of all the transactions we labeled as fraud. How many were actually frauds? Your accuracy may be high, but is it truly high? That's what precision answers in our scenario. The model identified under transactions as fraudulent, but only 80 are actually fraud. This means 20% of the time a legitimate transaction was incorrectly flagged as fraudulent. This would inconvenience customers. Right? Now let us look at recall. Recall is the true positive rate of all the fraudulent transactions. How many did we correctly identify? That is recall for you.

We got a recall score of 89%. What does it imply? Out of the 90 transactions that are actually fraudulent, the model was able to catch 80 of them. This means it missed ten transactions or 11% of fraudulent transactions. This could be a significant risk depending on the value of the claim. Finally, specificity. Specificity is true. Negative rate of all the legitimate transactions. How many of us correctly identified the model? 98% of the legitimate transactions. This is a good rate, but the 2% misclassification might still be a concern, especially if it leads to false alarms or blocked transactions for customers. So is this a good model? It is definitely an okay model and definitely a good model to start with. It offers a lot of opportunities to improvise further.

How to improve the accuracy of models

You can take a number of actions to improve the accuracy of the model, starting with increasing the data size. If the data size is small, algorithms typically tend to underperform. You can also add or remove some of the features in the model. You can also change the algorithms I mentioned about using logistic regression or decision tree. You can also try random forest or Xgboost. Random forest and Xgboost are very good algorithms and they are actually improvisations of the decision tree algorithm. If these don't work, we can fine tune the model by changing the values of hyperparameters. Thanks to the deployment, the General Insurance company for which the machine learning was deployed has managed to reduce the fraudulent claims by little under 10%. That is a very good start.

From Machine Learning to Deep Learning

The world of machine learning is actually giving way to deep learning where we can identify anomalies merely from images and chapters. What we saw earlier is tabular data, also known as structured data. We analyze structured data with the help of machine learning. Image analysis is best done. Using deep learning and deep learning is a more advanced form of machine learning. With the proliferation of mobile phones, the number of images has increased substantially and these images could be analyzed just like members to identify anomalies and potentially fraudulent claims. Unstructured data like images, audio and chapter files are handled with the help of a big data framework. But the algorithm we use in such scenarios is known as deep learning and specifically convolutional neural networks. Insurance companies have started to deploy visual inspection systems to identify anomalies or potentially fraudulent cases.

Explainable AI (XAI)

In this chapter, I want to touch upon a very important area known as explainable AI. When the model provides an output, the end users would like to know how the model has arrived at the prediction in a sensitive area like fraud. The question of how the model has identified a particular transaction as fraudulent has got deeper meaning. If I come and tell you that you are fraudulent, how will you feel if I accuse you of fraud? I have a responsibility to provide the reasoning. Without that reasoning, my trust will be reduced. This challenge is addressed by explainable AI, a budding area in machine learning. Machine learning models are like a black box. That is, we do not know how the algorithms identify something as an output or fraudulent in the fraud detection algorithm.

The way the algorithms identify the patterns are hidden from us. We call that a hidden layer in machine learning. Explainability is all about breaking down the black box nature of machine learning models and providing clarity on how they arrive at decisions. This includes knowing which features the data most influence the predictions, how each features values, impact predictions and understanding the overall logic. The model applies to making decisions. There are two aspects to interpretability: global as well as local insights derived from global and local interpretability approaches serve distinct objectives. Global interpretability fosters strategic decision making at an organizational level.

While local interpretability guides more targeted specific actions, let us say we are trying to predict employee churn by considering different factors like age performance rating, stock option level salary hike, distance from home. Employee satisfaction. Total years of work experience and few other factors. John, if you see, is primarily applied in the customer experience area and we use machine learning models to predict which of the customers are likely to churn or leave a service provider like telecom, financial and so on. We are now extending that concept to employee experience scenarios. So in an employee churn prediction scenario using machine learning, the list of employees likely to leave the organization is a good starting point to address churn.

But beyond that, the functional managers and the teams would like to know the factors of churn so that they could take action to address churn. So explainable AI helps us in such a scenario. It provides insights for both global as well as local interpretability. The explainable AI model identified monthly income as the primary factor driving employee churn, followed by training, age and stock option level. The rest of the factors are relatively of lower importance compared to the top factors. This is global interpretability for you. If we consider local interpretability for two different data points.

We observe that the influential factors dictating the decisions vary considerably. Interestingly, monthly income, which emerged as the most critical determinant in global interpretability, does not hold a significant role in shaping the decision for the first data point. This difference underlines the potency of explainable AI. With this level of insight, end users or operational teams can undertake precise evidence based actions to drive performance improvements. Such capability enhances the accuracy and the tailored application of AI decision making, thereby making it a critical asset in data driven operations.

Case Study 2: Sales & Supply Chain Demand Planning Analytics

In this chapter, we are going to look at time series forecasting. Time series forecasting predicts future values based on past and present data points in a chronological order. The chronological order is a necessary condition in time series forecasting. At the Heart of Time series forecasting lies Time Series analysis. Imagine a sequence of data points measured typically at successive points in time. This sequence provides us with invaluable insights into the potential future points. Econometric models took this a step further. They didn't just look at data. They combined economic theory with statistical methods. By representing economic relationships through equations, these models provided a structured way to understand and predict economic activity.

Then came a breakthrough. In the 70s, the Arima or Autoregressive integrated moving average model introduced by George Box and Jenkins, became a cornerstone in Time series forecasting. By considering the relationship between an observation and a number of lagged observations, Arima provided a robust way to predict future points in a series. . The world of forecasting saw the rise of exponential smoothing techniques. These methods gave more weight to recent observations. By doing so, they could adapt more quickly to changes, making them especially useful for business applications with evolving trends. As we moved into the 21st century, the explosion of data and computational power paved the way for machine learning and deep learning models.

Neural networks, with their ability to capture intricate patterns and relationships, became game changers. Techniques like long short term memory networks or revolutionized. Time series forecasting by recognizing long term dependencies in data. But as with all changes, forecasting is not static. Today we are witnessing a blend of traditional methods like Arima with cutting edge techniques. Hybrid models, which combine statistical methods with machine learning, are emerging as powerful tools. And as our models become more complex, there is a growing emphasis on making them understandable. This is where explainable AI or Xai comes into play.

In a world that is becoming increasingly data driven, it is not enough to have a model that is accurate. We need models that we can trust, models that can explain their predictions. Imagine you are listening to a symphony. Each instrument plays its part, contributing to the overall masterpiece. But what if you could isolate each instrument, sound, understand its rhythm, its highs and lows, and its contribution to the entire piece? This is precisely what we aim to do with Time series data through decomposition. Time series like the Symphony is a combination of several underlying patterns. At its core. Time Series Decomposition breaks the series into three primary components. Trend seasonality and residual. Seasonality represents the repeating short term cycle in the series.

It is the rhythmic pattern that occurs, be it daily, monthly, yearly or any other periodic cycle. For instance, ice cream sales might spike every summer and dip during winter. Recognizing the seasonality allows us to anticipate these regular fluctuations and plan accordingly. The trend is the long term movement in data. Think of it as the underlying trajectory of the data. Is it increasing, decreasing or staying relatively stable over time? Identifying the trend helps us to understand the general direction in which our data is moving. For example, if we are looking at a company's sales data, a rising trend might indicate overall growth in sales over the years. After accounting for the trend and seasonality, what remains is the residual.

It is the noise, the randomness and the unpredictability. It is the part of the data that the trend and seasonality components cannot explain. While it might seem just like noise, understanding residuals is crucial. They can sometimes hold insights into anomalies or events that aren't part of the regular pattern, like a sudden spike in sales due to a one time marketing event. Decomposition provides clarity by isolating each component. We can model them separately, tailoring our approach to each one's unique characteristics. For example, while we might use a linear or polynomial fit for the trend, we could employ a cyclical model for seasonality. By then, combining our forecast for each component, we achieve a more accurate and holistic prediction for the entire series.

Please note this process of decomposition aids immensely in anomaly detection as well. Now let us look at how a retail company took a leap in forecasting accuracy, driving significant improvements across their operations and business predictability. The six month forecast accuracy soared from the low 60s to an impressive mid. The three month forecast accuracy made an even more significant leap, moving from the low 80s to the high 90s. These aren't just numbers. They represent a paradigm shift in the approach. The initial forecasting model was heavily reliant on templates. While it served the company in the past, they recognized the need for a more dynamic, responsive and accurate system.

They considered various factors that influenced the sales, starting with seasonality inputs. Recognizing the cyclical patterns in consumer behavior throughout the year is very important. Using the past to predict the future is all about understanding the historical demand. Incorporating real time data from sales teams is always critical. The next is about production inputs, which gives insights about capacity and production nuances. Last but not the least, is operational inputs. We should always factor in the day to day realities of running a retail business. Recognizing the limitations of a one size fit all template the transition to a hybrid model. This model combined the strengths of traditional forecasting methods like Arima with the power of modern machine learning techniques.

The result is a system that was not only more accurate, but also more attuned to the complexities and nuances of the business. The benefits of this transformation were manifold. Starting with demand forecasting. The company could anticipate market demand with unprecedented precision. There was no more overstocking or under stocking. They achieved the Goldilocks principle just right. By understanding demand better. The drastically reduced instances where customers faced out-of-stock situations, enhancing their shopping experience and their brand reputation. But as with all great endeavors, this wasn't a journey they undertook alone.

They onboarded a dedicated five member demand forecasting team who were experts in supply chain analytics. Their mandate was clear dry forecasting using this new approach and providing actionable insights to the business units. Their expertise was invaluable bridging the gap between data technology and business needs. Furthermore, they recognize the importance of granularity. The forecasting was done at an SQL level every month, ensuring precision at the most granular level. These level forecasts were then aggregated, providing a comprehensive view at the organizational level. In conclusion, their journey in improving forecast accuracy wasn't just about numbers. It was about embracing change, leveraging technology and fostering collaboration.

Case Study 3: Image/chapter Analytics & Social Distance

The next case study that we are going to see is face deduction, as I explained in one of the previous chapters, for Face detection, we'll be using either image or chapter. And this comes under deep learning technology. Machine learning as such is used whenever numbers are there and deep learning is used when we have to work on images and chapters. Right. So in this case study that I'm showing here, this was done for a manufacturing organization and they wanted critical equipment to be handled only by authorized and also certified engineers. Being a new equipment and being a critical equipment, they did not want any kind of mishaps to happen. So we offered a deep learning based solution in which the face of the certified engineer is detected right .

The face of the engineer is detected and it is checked against the employee records. where, details of the certification is available. Whenever we face a problem, a non-certified employee is detected. The mismatch was highlighted and an email trigger was sent to the floor supervisor and the manager also. So this ensured that the only people who were certified ended up operating the critical equipment. Using this, we were also able to identify repeat offenders and thereby took some aggressive action. Right. There's a simple solution, but combined both IOT as well as deep learning. And through this solution, we were able to address the requirements of the organization. So I want to highlight that this face deduction can be applied across a broad spectrum of industries.

Right? Not just in a manufacturing equipment operating scenario. Right. Because essentially we were trying to ensure that the person who was authorized to use the equipment is actually using the equipment, so this is kind of intrusion detection so we can very well apply where surveillance and such kind of intrusion detection need to be monitored and alerted. We can use such face detection solutions. In the next case study. We will see how a deep learning solution was used for ensuring social distancing between two individuals in covid times. This is a critical requirement. In the previous case study, the validation was done based on an image of the employee here, also the image of the employee is what has been checked, but the input is actually coming from a live chapter feed.

The live chapter feed is fed into the deep learning solution, and the deep learning solution will identify whether any two individuals are maintaining the required social distance or not. Whenever the system identifies such breaches in terms of not maintaining the necessary social distancing and alarm is triggered through the IOT system. The alarm will be played in the area where such breaches are noted by the system. There's a very simple solution, but leveraging the power of. Deep learning technology. The organization is able to ensure. Adequate social distancing. Thanks to this solution.

Case Study 4: Outlier or Anomaly Detection

Outliers or anomaly detection is a wonderful area where I see a lot of action. It's also an area with a lot of potential. Anomaly is something that doesn't fit with the rest of the data set, like the red fish you see in this image. It is used in multiple areas, in multiple industries, from fraud detection, customer churn prediction to defaulters prediction. It is also useful in operations management, in proactively identifying warning signs, and this scenario can be applied to any type of industry. Just like with numbers, we can identify anomalies with images as well, we analyze images just like we can analyze numbers. Having seen that anomaly can be applied, let's understand this anomaly in detail. OK, what is this anomaly all about? So you can explore this in your organization.

I know you all understand about Outliers. As I said earlier, anomalies and outliers are one and the same. In these images that you are seeing on your screen, data points that correspond to change in direction or also outliers or anomalies. This probably would not be captured when you use Excel or simple applications that look at just percentages and percentiles, on the other hand, and AI based algorithms that understand the patterns comprehensively will be able to identify the anomalies or outliers better. Also, when your data set is small you can use Excel, probably plot a graph and identify outliers, but when data points are more you definitely need.

The AI based anomaly detection algorithms, another reason why you need AI based algorithms is when you have multiple factors, when you have a single factor or few factors, visualizing a set of data points is easier. But when you have, say, 10 or 20 parameters, how will you identify anomalies? You can't even visualize it, so you definitely need AI based algorithms. Since anomaly detection has wide applicability. I strongly encourage you to try this out.

Case Study 5: Customer Segmentation

If you're wondering how AI can help your company to grow the top line or make more revenue, look, no further AI is now being used in customer segmentation. We can identify new segments of customers and new segments means new products, new markets and obviously money. What you're seeing here is an example of customer segmentation done on just two parameters for an online store, annual income of customers and annual spend. Before the exercise, the company had three major customer groups to work with.

After this exercise, we identified new customer segments over and beyond the three major customer groups. This opened up new vistas for the company. Also, if this company were to consider additional factors like, say, sex and age of customers in addition to income and spend, we just can't use Excel or simple tools. We need algorithms that can dissect data at multiple dimensions and then identify the customer segments. Not just that the algorithms can even tell the factors that are important for each segment. That's a wealth of information for marketers and product developers.

Understanding the clustering algorithm

In this chapter, we will see the algorithm behind clustering k-nn and work by identifying the distance between a central point and the rest of the points in the data set. All data points with lower distance would form a cluster. The central point is chosen at random and we compute the distance between the central point and the rest of the points. The distance is computed using the Euclidean formula, which is the square root of x two minus x one. The whole square plus y two minus y one. The old square. Any two points in a cluster can be represented with the help of x y coordinates, namely x, one, y one and X2Y2. So we can very well use the Euclidean distance formula to measure the distance.

This is an example of a cluster with five nearest neighbors or K equals five. Now consider this scenario of age, height and weight. We have to predict the weight of the last person or the last data point. We will compute the distance between the last point and each of the other data points. This will be used to compute or predict the weight of the last person or the last data point. How will you arrive at the Euclidean distance for the first data point? It is already showing a value of 3.01. How did you arrive at this number? It is with the help of the Euclidean distance. It is six -5.8. The whole square plus 40, -37, the whole square. The result of this computation is 3.01.

Similarly, we compute the Euclidean distance between the last point and the rest of the data points. That is how we have computed the Euclidean distance for all the data points in our dataset except the last one. So the wait for the last person in our dataset will be the average of the three data points that are circled. I have considered a scenario of three nearest neighbors to the last data point, which is why I am taking the least distance.

Anomaly, Clustering and Forecasting with Power BI

In this chapter, I would like to demonstrate clustering. Time Series Forecasting and Anomaly detection using Power BI. Power BI is not just a data analysis or visualization tool. It is increasingly becoming an auto ML tool. Auto ML or automated machine learning is a process in which we accomplish the goals of machine learning without writing a single line of code. I am going to demonstrate using a simple dataset so that you understand the concept. Let us start with clustering. You can download the Power BI desktop version from online. The desktop version in fact is free to use. Whatever I am demonstrating is using the desktop version. So let us start by importing the dataset. Once you start Power BI, this is the view you get here. You can filter.

These are the visualizations that are available in Power BI. Once you load the dataset, you can see the dataset here, okay, all the fields will appear, the data itself will be available in the table view. Once I download, you will understand what I am talking about. So let us start by importing the data. You can import the data from multiple sources. I am going to take a simple Excel file. You can import your data from other sources too. For example, you can import from SQL, Oracle, IBM, MySQL databases. So many options are available as part of Power BI. I'm going to import from Excel. So let's click this. Let me choose the data that I want to bring into the Power BI environment. I'll click Open. Now Power BI is prompting whether it should load the data or it should transform the data and then load.

What is this data transformation? Sometimes when you bring the data from sources like Excel or databases like Oracle or MySQL, it can be any database for that matter. Some of the data may be lost. Some of the data may be corrupted, some of the fields may appear empty. In such situations, we must either remove those blank fields, we must remove those junk fields, or we must replace those null or junk values with some other value. That is data transformation. That is, I make the data ready to do the analysis, ready to do the visualization. Okay. Remember, Power BI is basically a visualization tool on top of it. The mission learning capabilities have been added. Okay, but data transformation is an important step in machine learning too.

When you have blank values, the machine learning algorithms, they won't work. Okay, so let's click load because we are not going to do any transformation. Once the data is loaded, the fields will appear in this area. Okay. It's getting loaded. Okay. The loading is complete. All the fields that are there in our dataset are appearing in this area. The data itself can be viewed in the table view. Okay. This contains. The data in our dataset. This displays the data in our dataset. Let's go and create the clustering now. Okay. This is the area where we are going to create the cluster. This phase is for filtering. If you want to filter any of the visualizations, you can add conditions in this area. Okay, let's start with a scatter chart. Scatter chart helps to create clusters.

We are going to create two dimensional clusters to start with. We are going to create clusters for annual income and age. So let's bring annual income to X axis and age to Y axis. We will bring customer ID the reference for each of the points in our dataset into the values column. So you can see here all the data points have been populated. Okay, Now what I'm going to do is I'm going to click the ellipses. Okay. The three dots. Once I click this, I have so many options. I can either export this data, I can see this in the form of a table. That is also one more option here. Automatically find clusters. Okay. When I click this power BI will run the necessary code in the back end. We won't see that code. But Paul will run the necessary code and provide the output for us. Just like how it ran the code and created this visual. Right.

How? How Power BI is created this visual. There is some programming, right? We don't get to see the programming. We just get to see the output. We chose the fields and we have the output. Similarly, I'm going to automatically select clusters. Okay. I've selected that option. I can either choose auto or I can even mention the number. Okay. Like two, three, four. That option is also there. Okay. But now I'm going to leave it to Power BI to determine the number of clusters. So let's click. Okay. We will see clusters appearing very shortly. Remember, we have created the clusters in two dimensions. So you can see it has identified three clusters. So these are the three clusters in our dataset. Okay. We have created these clusters in two dimensions, which is why I chose a scatter chart. Okay.

We have created the clusters for age and annual income, but there is one more information that could be used to create a cluster which is a pending score. Okay. I cannot create a cluster or a scatter chart with three dimensions. How can I visualize a cluster in three dimensions? I cannot use a visual like this. I have to use a table. Are you able to understand what I'm trying to say? I visualize this in the form of a chart because there are only two dimensions here. If I add more dimensions, I can only see the output in the form of a table. I cannot visualize it in the form of a chart like this. Okay. Since I want to consider the spending score, I will use the table visual. Okay, let's minimize this and drag it towards the top. Okay, now let's click the table visual. Let's put it here. The table we shall have chosen. Let's make this slightly bigger.

We will bring the necessary fields into this column. We will bring age. Let's first bring a customer ID. Okay. Let me unselect that customer ID. Age. Annual income and spending score. Okay. So you see, only one row is appearing. We need to choose. Don't summarize. Then all the fields, that is, all the rows appear. Now let's click the three ellipses, three dots. The ellipses option here automatically finds clusters. And this time let me indicate four. So I want to find four clusters. I'll click. Okay. And now that cluster information. Gets added as an additional column. Can you see here it gets added as an additional column. Right. Now I want to find the characteristics of the cluster. What is the average age? What is the average income? What is the average spending score in each of the clusters so that I can make some decisions, and I can drive some marketing campaigns? How will I do that? I will create another table. Okay, let's create another table.

This time I'm going to bring a cluster ID here. Okay. This is the second cluster. Remember, this one corresponds to the cluster here. Okay, so let's click this. That is, we bring it into the column area. See, there are four clusters. We will bring age. Annual income and spending score. Okay, so what you see is sum instead of sum, let me choose average. I can choose minimum maximum variation. I can choose any of the parameters there. They are known as descriptive statistics. Okay. What you see here is nothing but descriptive statistics. Let's choose average here as well. On average here as well. Okay, so now I have the information for each of the clusters. That is, I have summarized the characteristics of the cluster in this table. Let me arrange the table so that you can see that clearly.

I will move this here. Know that here. And then let me adjust the size of the table. Okay. So I've adjusted. I will do the same here as well. Okay. Maybe I'll put this below and I will move this here. Okay. So I will use the rest of the area for the other tasks. That is, remember, we wanted to do forecasting and anomaly detection as well. So we will use this space to create visuals and analysis outcomes for forecasting and anomaly detection. Let me adjust the size of the column so you can see clearly. Our largest for annual income and spending score as well. So have adjusted so we can see the information clearly. Okay. I want to do some basic formatting. Okay, let me select this. Come here format your visual.

General visual. Okay, Click effects. I want to show a visual border. Okay. Let me select one and see where the border appears for this visual. I will do the same thing for this as well. Come to General Effects. Visual border. We will choose one. Okay. So it is clear. Okay, the visual is very clear to see and distinguish. Now let us import the file for forecasting and anomaly detection. I once again have to click get data, choose Excel because I'm going to be using Excel. This is a CSV file. I'll click that and then I will choose the necessary folder. So I choose the file that I want to use. I'll click open. Power BI will prompt again whether it should be loaded or transformed and then loaded. So I'm going to click load.

Let's click that. The data is getting loaded and once it is loaded, the fields in that file will appear in this area. Okay. Just like a cluster. Let's click this and see why this is a date column. And this is a numeric column. Here, if you see Power BI did not pick the date correctly. It identified years here as a numeric column. That is why this sigma notation is appearing. Okay. Here if you see sigma notation is not appearing, it means it is a non numeric data. Power BI is correctly identified as a binary type of data. Male female as the output. Okay. But in this case Power BI is identified as a date column. We did not use EOR while creating the cluster. If you have to use it here, we have to necessarily transform the data, that is, convert the data from numeric to a date column. Okay.

That is part of data transformation. So now coming to this data set, let's see what is there in the data. So it contains. This is the old one. Okay, let's click this profit. Remember, I'm using the word profit. Is there any significance for it? Yes, there is a significance. Profit is a very powerful library or algorithm from Facebook. It combines the best of traditional methods and also deep learning techniques. When I say traditional, I'm referring to Arima. That is the Autoregressive integrated moving average model. Profit combines Arima with some of the deep learning models and the accuracy of the profit model is very high. That is why I've named the file as profit. So this is the date and the sales information. The daily sales information is available. We want to use Power BI to predict the future sales.

So let's go to the visualization area. We will click the line chart. Okay, so we'll first create a line chart and then incorporate forecasting in there. So let's drag the DS to the x axis that is the date column and Y2Y axis. Okay, let us unselect the date hierarchy so that we are able to see all the data points. Okay. Now to do the forecasting. I choose to add further analysis to your visual option. You see many options here as part of adding further analysis. I am interested in the forecast, so let me enable the forecast and indicate that I need a forecast for 365 data points. 365 data points correspond to 365 days in a year. For the rest of the details, I will go with the default options. Confidence Interval tells What is the level of confidence that I have in this particular model. Seasonality is something that gets repeated every year.

For example, sales increase during the Christmas or holiday season and sales drop during the off season period. If you want to ignore certain points, you can ignore that as well. Okay, but for now, I'm going to go with the default options. I click apply and I have the forecast in front of me. The forecast contains the forecasted value and also lower bound and upper bound. What does it indicate? Normally forecasts are provided as part of a range. You provide the upper value and the lower value. Whenever you talk about the forecast, if I say how many marks you will get in an exam, you will probably say I will score between 70 to 80. So that 70 to 80 is your range. You may probably end up with 73 or 76. So the forecast is normally provided with a range of information and power BI provides that detail as well.

So we have completed the cluster as well as forecasting. What is left is anomaly detection. Before adding an anomaly, I want to add a title to this dashboard. This is the dashboard, right? We did a lot of visuals, a lot of analysis, but this is basically a dashboard. As I said earlier, Power BI is basically a visualization tool. So how can I add a title? I can choose a text box. Okay, I will call this cluster and. Forecasting. Let's start with a cluster. And forecasting. Let me do some basic formatting for this. I will center this and choose a dark color. Blue color. Okay, we'll go with blue color and we will choose a light color font so that this is. Clearly visible, we will increase the font size. Also, we'll choose an 18 size. Okay, that looks good. And we will drag this. Here. Okay. And we will widen this as well. So you have a title for the dashboard? Okay.

This looks neat, right? Let's bring this down a bit. We will also bring this down. We have adjusted. Let's also have a border for this. Effects. Visual border on. Okay. So that it is neat. It's not going to take a lot of time, but let's do this. Now to demonstrate anomaly detection, I will first bring the data into the Power BI environment. We are considering a banking scenario, so the file contains date and transaction value information. So this is also a CSV file. CSV file occupies less space compared to XLS format. So we are going to load the data and not do any transformation. So let me click load. Once the loading process is complete, the fields in that file will appear in this space. Okay, let's wait for that process to be complete. Yes, that process is complete. We can see the date and the transaction value information. Let's create a line chart similar to the earlier one. Let's make this bigger.

I'm going to drag data into the x axis and transaction value into y axis, and I'm going to change the hierarchy so that all the data points are displayed. Now I'm going to the Add further analysis area. Enable anomalies and power. BI has identified the anomaly for us. It also tells why this is an anomaly point. Okay. It says the expected value is 9.86, whereas the actual value is 12.1 and hence it is an anomaly. So that way Power BI makes anomaly detection a rather smooth process. It identifies anomalies pretty fast and it also tells why it is an anomaly. So some elements of explainable AI are available in power BI as well. Let's also create a border for this for completeness sake. Effects. Visual border. Let's click on it. Okay. Let's make this slightly bigger. Shall we increase the font size? Yeah.

Let's slightly increase the font size. Right. So you have the dashboard. So we took, what, about 20 minutes? We have the visuals, we have everything for us. You can publish this dashboard as a web link, and this can be viewed in mobile as a mobile application. So those are the opportunities with Power. BI I feel Power BI is uniquely positioned to take advantage of the machine learning market. It is because the output of any data analysis, any machine learning algorithm has to be in the form of tables and visualizations because the end audience will consume the outcome and output of your analysis in the form of visuals, graphs and tables. So that way Power BI is advantageous. What I demonstrated is all part of the power BI free version, advanced machine learning and deep learning algorithms are also possible in power BI and they are available only for the paid version.

Case Study 6: Predictive Maintenance

In this chapter, we're going to see a case study on predictive maintenance. Here we are talking of preventing prediction. Then I said, preventive, it's about doing maintenance at regular intervals, like when you have a automobile, right, like a motorbike or a car, you will do service, planned service after a certain usage or after a certain period of time. That is what you do. Preventive maintenance. where as in predictive maintenance. You do some intervention activity based on the performance of the mission. Can you see this, can visualize the image that is there. This is a cooling tunnel That is there in large establishments in an industrial establishment, if the cooling tower is not working on a critical machinery, it is not working.

The factory cannot produce its product. If the products are not produced, they cannot be sold. So there is a financial impact to everything. That's what we are trying to reduce or avoid using the concept of predictive. So, as I said, you are seeing huge machinery on your screen. See if the performance of such a large equipment, if it can be monitored at a granular level. It can. throw out a lot of information and using that information, you can take proactive action. So the entire idea of preventive maintenance can become predictable. That's what we are aiming for, in Industry 4.0 and that is a possibility in industrial analytics. OK, and as I said earlier. Before the advent of the sensors, the smart sensors.

People were not measuring the performance of the equipment regularly. They will probably measure the performance of such a large equipment. OK, say once a month. What happens after taking the measurement, something drastic happens to the equipment is going to lead to a shutdown, right? If it is critical equipment. Because of the advancement of sensor technology, right, you are able to measure, as I said earlier, not just industrial establishments, all walks of life, this level of measurement has not happened. And because we are capturing so much information that information can be processed and analyzed intelligently for proactive actions. So that's the possibility and that's how the close looping happens.

So far, such a large piece of equipment. The key parameters that you typically measure are temperature, pressure, speed, vibration, age of the machine. Type of the machine. So these are the typical parameters, and if it is throwing up information in regular intervals, if it is critical equipment, we can even measure the performance at a second level. every second it can throw up. Information about its performance like what is the temperature, what is the pressure, what is the speed? All that information, the machine can throw up, right? And once that information is there, you can take action. Based on intelligent analysis, and that analysis is based on machine learning technology, right? So in the opportunity that is there, right.

You can maximize the uptime of critical equipment. Of course, there will be redundancies, but still it makes sense to ensure that the critical equipment uptime is optimized, predicted on equipment that is monitored manually, there will be many equipment where the monitoring is manual. There are no sensors. Also, predictive maintenance can help. Right. More importantly, in all these machineries. The failure will happen once in a blue light, but when it happens, the impact is huge. Right. That's the challenge in an industrial establishment. If you typically see an industrial establishment that is maintained, well, reasonably well, failures don't happen, normally don't happen, big failures are rare, but when it happens, the impact is huge.

Right, it can lead to even loss of lives in an industrial establishment. because it can trigger a fire accident or, you know, harmful chemicals can be released in gas. So it is important that the industrial establishments and factories always stay one step ahead of the game. Right, and that's a possibility in predictive maintenance. In fact, by using predictive maintenance, people have been able to bring down the instances of downtime by as much as two thirds. OK, because there are existing tools like non destructive testing, statistical process control, but they are still not. Predicted they are not truly proactive. True prevention happens when you can analyze the information that your machinery is throwing into an application system, you analyze that.

And from that, you identify the critical areas and go and take proactive actions in those areas. Right, and the other possibilities are very useful for companies that don't have historical failure information. Many times companies don't have historical failure information or very little failure information. As I said, the occurrence of failure is limited. If somebody captures say 10000 data points, there'll be just one failure. So how will you identify a pattern? Do you understand the challenges now in a real life scenario? I know we explain pattern recognition rather easily. But when you come to a practical, real life scenario. It is very different. In an industrial establishment, you have 10000 data points. But there is just one failure or two failures.

So how will your system even identify a pattern? Because there is no pattern, right? How can your software identify a pattern? So that's where experience counts. That's where your knowledge, solid understanding of these technologies matter. Right. So these are the kind of practical challenges that machine learning experts will face. And it's one thing to know in theory, another thing to apply in real life scenarios. But understand that predictive maintenance is a fabulous concept that is used now, right, in fact it's been around now with more interconnected devices, more measurements, people are doing intelligent analysis, identifying patterns, and people are taking proactive actions and downtime of large equipment.

Critical equipment is coming down. Yes, this is going to cost money for an industrial establishment and they cannot afford it for all equipment because you will have a lot of equipment in an industrial establishment. But this can be applied to critical equipment. You can apply predictive maintenance even to an air conditioning system at home. But does it make economic sense? The answer is no. Right, because the cost of deploying a system, because the cost of the system itself, right. It doesn't make sense at all. So all these things are to be factored right before you decide a strategy. But predictive maintenance is sweeping the world, the industrial world, and it's helping to bring down the instances of downtime. So what you see is a predictive maintenance tool OK, so what you see here This is a motor. motorized equipment.

It is pumping different chemicals in a process industry. It's pumping different chemicals, so the industrial motors, right? Their performance is critical if they don't pump the chemicals right in the right quantity, it can cause problems. This is applicable in the oil and gas industry because the oil needs to be pumped from the oil well. The motor that you see right in our house or an apartment complex, right? That is not an industrial pump. Here we are talking of an industrial park, right, that can pump different types of fluids. At different speeds. OK, the asset performance. You monitor temperature pressure age, you can have multiple parameters, depending on what you want to monitor, right. So using all of this.

The system can tell with a precision right on this day, you are likely to have an incident. What you are seeing here, the historical data was set for January to August 2018. The output shows likely repair events for September to December 2018. So for the period of September to December, the system tells when the future failure is going to happen. As I said, this is used. this is a real life scenario, what you're seeing on your screen is a real life scenario. The software predicts when future failure can happen and there's a wealth of information for the floor managers, the factory managers, they can take action, they can take proactive actions. Right. I hope you're able to understand how these concepts are applied in real life. OK, so as I said, it's used to improve productivity and as productivity improves, economic value improves. Which are. objective anyway OK.

Decision Tree

The algorithm that was used in predictive maintenance, which we saw earlier, is . It is based on the Decision Tree. I wanted to provide some additional details about this algorithm and also cover important topics relevant to machine learning, like variance, bias, trade off. So we will start this chapter with Decision Tree and then get into Xgboost. We will take up a health care scenario to explain the Decision Tree. A decision tree is a supervised machine learning algorithm used for classification and regression tasks. It is also used in data analysis extensively. It works by splitting the data into subsets based on the values of input features. Creating a tree-like model of decisions.

This approach is intuitive and easy to visualize. Making decision trees a popular choice for both beginners as well as experts. Let us consider a health care scenario. We are trying to predict heart disease and we are considering three factors: blood pressure, sugar and cholesterol. The challenge in Decision Tree is where will you start from? That is what should be the root node. Will you start the tree with blood pressure or sugar or cholesterol? And what is the rationale for the decision? We use the concept of Gini index for deciding the root node. We can also use other methods like entropy. I am going to demonstrate using the Gini index. Someone with high BP is not high. BP is indicated by true and false respectively in the limbs.

Someone with high BP could develop heart disease or stay healthy. That is, yes and no. So someone with high developing heart disease is 105 and someone not developing heart disease is 39. Similarly, someone not having high BP, but developing heart disease is 34 and not developing heart disease is 125. These numbers come from the historical data in our dataset. We construct similar trees for sugar and cholesterol. Let me demonstrate how to calculate the Gini index for high scenarios. Gini index is calculated using the Formula one minus probability of s, the whole square minus probability of no, the whole square. For the true scenario, the value of the Gini index is one minus one zero five divided by 105 plus three nine.

The old squire -39 divided by 105 plus 39. The old Squire 105 plus 39. Total of 144. This results in a value of 0.395. Similarly, I calculate the Gini index for the false scenario. The Gini index for the false scenario would be one -34 divided by 34 plus 125. The old squire -125 divided by 34 plus 125. The old Squire. This results in a value of 0.336. We then combine the true and false scenarios. That is, basically do a weighted average of true and false scenarios to arrive at the total Guinea for high. This results in a value of 0.364. I computed a similar Gini index for sugar and cholesterol. I get a value of 0.36 for sugar and 0.381 for cholesterol. The node with lowest Gini index goes to the root node.

In this case it will be the sugar. That means the decision tree will start with sugar as the root node. In the primary stages of predictive modeling. Decision Trees played a pivotal role owing to their simplicity and interpretability. However, they are notoriously known to overfit the data, meaning that they are great at learning from the training data set but poor at generalizing to new unseen data. This is where ensemble methods like bagging and boosting come to rescue. At their heart, they work by combining the predictions from multiple models to improve the overall performance. The concept of bagging is used in random forests and the concept of boosting is used in .

Two most popular machine learning techniques of today are bootstrap. Aggregating is a parallel ensemble method. It involves creating multiple subsets of the training dataset using sampling with replacement and then training a model on each subset. The final prediction is obtained by averaging the predictions. For regression problems and voting for classification problems. The flagship algorithm using bagging is random forest, which leverages a forest of decision trees to arrive at prediction. By doing so, it not only overcomes the tendency of decision trees to overfit, but also brings in stability and reduction in variance in predictions. On the other hand, we have a sequential ensemble method.

It starts with a weak model and iteratively improves it by giving more weight to the instances that are wrongly predicted in the previous iterations. This forces the model to learn from mistakes, thereby reducing bias. The standout star in the boosting category is Xgboost, which has been a part of winning solutions in many machine learning competitions worldwide. It builds strong predictive models with high precision. We consider bagging to have an upper hand in terms of being faster and less prone to overfitting due to parallel training of models at the same time. Boosting though it is slower due to sequential training often results in more powerful models with higher predictive accuracy. However, boosting does come with a caution sign of a higher tendency to overfit, especially with noisy data.

While explaining, bagging and boosting, I kept referring to two terms: bias and variance. Let us understand the two as these two errors have an important role in machine learning. Bias refers to the error due to overly simplistic assumptions in the learning algorithm leading to underfitting. It is the difference between expected prediction and the actual. Variance refers to the error due to too much complexity in the learning algorithm leading to overfitting. It represents the model sensitivity to fluctuation in the training dataset. That is how much the predictions for a given point vary between different realizations of the model. In a high bias scenario, the model makes strong assumptions about the underlying distribution of the data and ignores the finer details, thus failing to capture the true relationship in a high variance scenario.

The model captures too much detail, including noise in the data, fitting too closely to the particulars of the training data and failing to generalize well to new and unseen data. In a low bias scenario, the model has a good balance and makes fairly accurate predictions by capturing the general trends in the data without focusing too much on the specifics. In a low variance scenario. On the other hand, the model doesn't change much with different sets of training data. It captures the essential patterns but not the noise, resulting in a more robust, generalizable model. A high bias can cause the model to miss relevant relations between features and target outputs, leading the model to be oversimplified.

A high variance can cause the model to model the random noise in the training data, leading the model to be overly complex. Imagine trying to shoot arrows at a target and all your arrows landing in roughly the same spot. But the spot is far from the center of the target. Your shots are consistent, but inaccurate. Now imagine your arrows landing all over the place, but with no discernible pattern. Your shots are inaccurate because they are influenced by many random factors. Despite having the correct aim on average, bias and variance represent two types of errors in models. Finding the right trade off between the two, which is often referred to as the bias variance Trade off is a fundamental task in machine learning as it helps us to create models that generalize well to unseen data by balancing complexity and simplicity. Key bias and variance in mind. As we explore Decision Tree, Random Forest and Xgboost.

NLP (Natural Language Processing)

NLP, as you can see here, is the intersection of three disciplines: computer science, artificial intelligence and human language. At its core, NLP is about how to program and analyze natural language data. When I say natural language data, I'm referring to the way you and I speak, right. That is the human language, we anyway have to do programming. Only then this process can be automated and we will be borrowing. The concepts of artificial intelligence, things like pattern recognition and machine learning and deep learning. So that's why this is at the intersection of three disciplines. NLP is concerned with the interactions between computers and human language.

When humans interact with one another, we are using language, right? So the system is going to engage just like a human being, understand the language and it is going to provide meaningful inferences to us. That's what makes NLP a very, very interesting field. So what are the applications of NLP? As I said, NLP. Is a very, very interesting area. It is used. In doing sentiment analysis, if you are getting feedback from customers, you want to know to what extent the feedback is positive, and to what extent the feedback is negative that can be done automatically using an NLP application. the world of chatbots, right.

It is based on NLP, right? Because in chatbot you are engaging with customers, you're talking, you're chatting with the bot. Right. All that is NLP. An interesting area that is emerging of late is how to convert speech to text, right? You can even analyze what is being said, right? So the speech is converted to text and that is analyzed. So that is also an application of NLP. Spam detection, in emails. We get a lot of spams. NLP can very easily and very effectively identify spam mails and filter them out. Right. Autofill that you are seeing here, you type the part of the word. the system guesses as to what it is that you are trying to type. OK, so that's autofill that is also based on. NLP. last but not the least when you have a document and you want important information culled from the document. Right.

Important information like name and other details. That is also NLP. what is called entity recognition. We'll be seeing that in the Book of the chapter. Right. If you see in this image. Right. I want my name, my organization, people whom I like and where I'm from all this information to be culled on. OK, so all these are wonderful application areas. And the key point to note, this technology is alive and kicking. You're not talking of a technology that's going to be there in future. It's already there and it's deployed at scale in many organizations. So when I say scale, I'm saying I'm emphasizing that we are not talking of applications that are deployed on proof of concept scenarios. These are being tested and are now in full blown applications.

Having seen what is NLP and what are the implications of NLP, let us quickly understand one of the challenges in NLP, OK? If somebody says, I want all the restaurants within a five mile or five kilometer radius, I'm referring to restaurants right here, the word restaurant is explicitly mentioned. On the other hand, if I say show me some close by, locations close by, places to eat, I'm still referring to restaurants . The third option, display food places nearby. I'm referring to restaurants again, so my system should be able to understand these different scenarios like I currently suggest. What is it that I am looking for in this case , restaurants? Right. So NLP involves addressing these challenges. So this is the challenge and also an opportunity. Right. Depends on how you look at it.

Case Study 7: Speech to Text

In this chapter, we are going to see the application of speech to text technology. In action. This scenario is very much applicable in the call center industry. In a call center industry, customers would call the call center either to resolve issues or to seek information about product or service. After the call is completed. The recorded calls are again listened to by quality control executives, and they will validate the call on multiple parameters. In fact, if you see the call center industry, there is an army of people who are doing this checking because the call centers want to ensure the customer has a positive experience. But this manual process can be automated thanks to the advances in technology. We can convert the recorded call. It can be a MP4 or MP3 file into text. And once the text is converted, we can analyze the text using NLP technology.

OK, so in this chapter, I'm going to demonstrate a Web application that we did for one of our customers. The customer can upload the file and see whether specific parameters have been compiled or not. In this demonstration, I'm going to show whether the. Customer service executive or the call center greeted the customer or not .Normally as part of the quality control process, multiple parameters are checked, but I'm just going to demonstrate one parameter, OK? So this is the Web application. The customer will choose the files here. Let's choose the fines and I can upload any one of the files. I'm just uploading a sample,

OK? And then I click open and the file has been selected and now I will submit it for analysis. So this is a wav file OK.

Remember I said it can be an MP3 or MP4 file also that different formats can also be supported through this technology. And once the file has been uploaded, the system will process and tell whether the greeting is there or not. See here. Yes, it says the greeting is then I can also download this right. Has an Excel fight. You see this Excel file is there. Right. And, the Excel file can further be analyzed also. That is the advantage with this technology. Now let's see one more sample, right? I'll take this file, synthesize it. See this here also the greeting is there. OK, and again, I can download this for further analysis. OK, and if you see these two cases that I just demonstrated, the greeting was there, and in fact, in these two examples, the customer service executive was an Indian and hence the voice was also of Indian accent.

The third custody, which was an interaction which was handled by an American customer service executive that means the accent is American. The technology supports different accents. And that's an advantage. Right? In fact, it's a necessity. Because different customer service executives will have different accents. I uploaded the file, but unfortunately, in this case, the greeting is not there. OK, I can download this again. For further analysis. Cool right, and once they have the Excel files, I can do other types of analysis also. Right. So this is an application of speech to text technology in action.

Evolution of ChatGPT

Before exploring more topics related to ChatGPT and generative AI. I would like to quickly summarize the developments that have happened in the last one year in generative AI. It's been a busy year for technology. The decades have indeed happened in the last few months. The landscape of artificial intelligence has rapidly evolved, with generative AI becoming a cornerstone of this transformation. ChatGPT is at the forefront of these advancements. Here is a glimpse of how ChatGPT and generative AI have progressed in the last 11 months, a period bustling with innovation. OpenAI introduced ChatGPT in November 2022, taking a significant step in making conversational AI more interactive and user friendly. Around the same time, a tool named Midjourney emerged for image generation, showcasing the potential of combining textual and visual elements in AI computing.

Solutions like Google's Bard were introduced, indicating a growing interest in generative AI. OpenAI launched the ChatGPT API along with GPT four, making it easier for developers to integrate and enhance their applications. ChatGPT plus was also introduced, offering a premium service with additional features. The period also saw the introduction of open source models like llama from meta, fostering an environment of collaborative innovation. The rollout of the ChatGPT plugin store and data analysis tools provided more control and customization to users, making the platform more versatile. These enhancements facilitated a richer interaction with AI, broadening its utility.

ChatGPT expanded its capabilities to include image generation, which is a major step in blending textual and visual AI. The introduction of multimodal ChatGPT combined text and image generation, showcasing the versatile potential for integrated solutions. So in the next chapter, we are going to see these recent advancements in detail with specific use cases.

Recent Advances in ChatGPT with Use Cases

In this chapter, I want to demonstrate the recent advances in ChatGPT. Let us start with advanced data analysis. This option used to be called a code interpreter. Some time back you can see the name code interpreter in the web link or the URL at the top. Once you select the Advanced Data Analysis option, you will see the plus sign appearing in your prompt area. You can upload your Excel file and do all the necessary analysis. Let us upload an insurance data set. This file has been uploaded and is now ready for analysis. The file contains insurance charges and the corresponding details for age, sex, smoking status, body mass index or BMI and region.

All these factors influence the outcome, that is, insurance charges, insurance companies evaluate the risk profile of an individual before issuing a term policy. That is, they assess whether the individual will live long enough if the risk to die early is high. The premium is kept at a higher level if the risk of dying early is lower. The premium is also kept lower in some rare cases. An insurance company may even deny issuance of a policy. That is, the insurance company can refuse to cover your risk. Now let us ask ChatGPT to do some analysis for us. We will start with the prompt, which is the most important factor in determining the insurance charges.

This is a very important aspect of any analysis. If you know what is causing a problem or what is driving an improvement, you can control or try to influence that variable or factor. In this scenario, knowing the key factor will help us to understand the dynamics of how insurance charges are determined in an insurance company. Many factors would influence an outcome, but there are always 1 or 2 factors that have a higher influence. So let us click enter and see the response from ChatGPT. Firstly, ChatGPT has correctly identified the data and factors in the data set. This is very important right now. Coming to the question I asked to answer that question, the analysts are ChatGPT. This case should know what are the factors influencing the outcome.

That is, the name of the factors and where they are available are paramount only. Only with this information can anyone do any type of analysis. ChatGPT has identified the technique that will be used to answer the question. Regression is the right technique. Correlation analysis using regression will help to provide the right insights to answer the question. It goes ahead with the analysis process and begins to calculate the correlation coefficient for each variable. ChatGPT refers to correlation coefficient as correlation in its response. It has computed the correlation coefficient value for each of the numeric variables. As per this, age seems to have a higher influence in our dataset. We also have non-numeric factors like sex, smoker status and region.

We should analyze those factors also, right? That is what ChatGPT is going to do now. However, we can't compute correlation coefficients for non-numeric variables like regions. To overcome this limitation, we have to first convert the non-numeric variables to numeric variables and then compute the correlation coefficient. This process of converting non numeric variables to numeric one is known as encoding. So ChatGPT is going to encode and then do the regression analysis for the converted data. We now have the correlation coefficient for each of the variables. And the conclusion is that smoker status is the most important variable, that is, whether an individual is a smoker or not plays a very important role in determining the quantum of charges. Other factors also play a role, but smoker status has a higher weightage.

So ChatGPT is not only doing analysis but also providing insights. So ChatGPT is your data analyst or business analyst or management consultant? I will leave it to you to figure out the answer. Now I would like to summarize the results in the form of visuals. After all, a picture is worth a thousand words. So ChatGPT lists the visuals that can be used in answering the question. Remember, our original question is which factor is influencing the insurance charges the most? ChatGPT plots a histogram and even infers the visual for us. It correctly points out that the data is clustered around the lower end, and that there is a noticeable right skew. It now plots a box plot and another box plot.

It also plots a regression chart along with these issues along with these visuals. It also provides the results of the analysis. So how did ChatGPT do all these analyses? It used Python to do the analysis. ChatGPT wrote the code for our custom, ran the code in the background and provided the analysis results. All these are Python code. In this case it is just a few lines of code. But to arrive at the answer, ChatGPT would have written at least 100 lines of code. You can do all these analyses in Excel, or even use a business intelligence tool like Tableau or Power BI. But ChatGPT makes the whole process a breeze. Just ask and you have the answer. That is all. It can even do pre-processing of data.

What is pre-processing? Before you can do any analysis, you need to clean the data and make it ready for analysis. Such tasks also can be done by ChatGPT. No more complaints from your data analysts. But do you need data analysts or business analysts in future? That is a fundamental question for you to ponder. There is, however, one big problem with using ChatGPT for your analysis. What is that? Think. It is data privacy. Will your data be safe when you upload the data? Is there a way out of the privacy issues? Well, there is, and we will discuss that in our subsequent chapters. Now let us get into the world of plugins. Once I enable the plugin option, I can access the numerous plugins available via the plugins.

Two plugins are like mobile applications in your Android or iPhone. Let us click Plugin Store and see what is in store for us. There are different tabs for new, installed, popular and all plugins. You can also search the plugin store. Plugins use the ChatGPT technology and provide us with options that are not provided by ChatGPT. We are going to see one such use case now, and the plugin I am going to use is diagrams to show me. This is already installed by me in my ChatGPT system. That is why you see the uninstall option there. Make sure that the plugin you are going to work with is enabled.

I am going to prompt ChatGPT to create a block diagram to assess risk profiles of people based on blood pressure, cholesterol, and sugar values.

If the values are above a certain threshold, the risk has to be categorized as high. If it is not, then it has to be marked as low. If at least one of the factors is below the threshold, the individual should be categorized as having medium risk. This is fairly straightforward, right? Let us see the response. Corporate world prefers block diagrams and it is an easy way to communicate. So here we are asking ChatGPT to create a block diagram with the information we just provided. So ChatGPT is working to get us the result. We have a simple block diagram as the response. Are you happy with this? I am not. So I'm going to ask again. This time we will ask the plugin to create a decision tree. It is the right way to represent risk assessment. Let us see the response this time around.

So it is working in the background. Please note that many of these plugins are also work in progress, just like ChatGPT, and you must be wary of privacy issues as well, so don't input anything confidential. We now have a decision tree. It is just about okay for me. In fact, it looks amateurish to me. We need the decision box in this diagram. The diamond shaped object. We accept that this is work in progress and we will move on. You can explore other plugins that help to create block diagrams like these in the plugin store. Can you see that there is an option to edit the diagram too? That will happen in their website and not in the Chat GPs work area. Now let us see image creation. This is done using Dal. So let us click that and enable the feature. Let us give a prompt on sarcasm.

Let us ask ChatGPT to create an image displaying sarcasm in a corporate or office setting. That is what we want. Sarcasm is not good for relationships, be it personal or professional. Yet many people display this. We see a lot of sarcasm these days in the corporate world. Let's wait for a few moments to see the results. Wow. We have four images. This is actually quite good, right? And the quantity of images is also good. Why do you need designers now? Well, that's a question for you to consider. Actually, there are many plugins available in the plugin store, and these plugins will convert the generated images into short chapters. Go ahead and explore them. Finally, the most impressive of all. We can now upload images and ask ChatGPT to interpret.

Once you are in default mode, this option appears. You can attach images. I'm going to attach an MRI scan image of the human brain and ask ChatGPT to interpret it. We got the disclaimer from ChatGPT and it is asking us to consult a medical professional. Let us continue the prompting process and ask again. Let us emphasize that this is for educational purposes only. Will we get a response this time? Let us see. Yes, we have got a response this time around. Lots of useful and technical information about the uploaded image. A non-medical professional like me cannot make use of this information anyway. I would like to ask the acid test question. Are there any abnormalities like tumors in the image? Let us re-emphasize that this is for educational purposes only.

I'm sure that you would agree with me that we must consult a qualified medical professional for scenarios like the one we are exploring. It is fun and educational, but we can't use the information from here to make decisions. So we hear the good news that there is nothing abnormal. What other use cases can you think of? I uploaded an image of a website and asked ChatGPT to give me the code. It actually provided the code not fully, but most of it. Any website will have images and many of them will be protected by copyright laws. So ChatGPT rightfully won't give those images. What ChatGPT will instead give is codes for layout, style, and color combinations. Finally, I want to demonstrate the use of browsing capabilities in ChatGPT.

This feature was not there earlier. Let us first enable the browsing option. I'm going to ask ChatGPT to provide a summary of recent developments in generative AI by browsing the internet. Note that I am indicating the developments in the last three months. De first sets up the browsing environment. He then starts browsing. It searches for websites like mckinsey.com. It even reads Forbes.com. And then we have the results clearly summarized as bullet points, along with clickable references provided as superscripts. How wonderful. Right? We have seen some fabulous use cases in this chapter. Now to the code posted. Can ChatGPT replace humans? My answer is a clear no. It can improve productivity and creativity. But is it going to replace human beings? Definitely not. And we are definitely not at that stage. We are still in the realm of we only.

Data Privacy for the ChatGPT World

In this chapter. Let us understand the data privacy issues that could arise by the use of artificial intelligence tools like Chatgpt. Tools like Chatgpt are trained on the data that is available on the Internet. So it is essentially public data that you and I have created. Data that you and I have left on the Internet. Chatgpt. Continuously improves itself, continuously trains itself with our data. When I say our data, I'm referring to the data that we leave with ChatGPT in the form of questions and the subsequent responses. So if your organization. If your team members are using chat GPT you must be aware of the privacy issues. Your team members could be using Chat Gpt to write emails, to create presentations and to generate content. To even write software code. Many of these.

Work that talked about. May have confidentiality requirements. Once you have fit data into ChatGPT, it is no longer private and confidential. So you must keep these things in your mind. The first and foremost action that you can take is to monitor the usage, continuously, assess the content that is being developed with the help of Chatgpt for originality requirements and copyright issues. The next one is about creating a list of acceptable tools to your organization. The number of tools that leverage the power of Chatgpt is increasing day by day, and it will definitely be confusing to your teams. So create a whitelist. Create a list of approved tools so that your team can make appropriate decisions. Regular training and audit is a must. Since this is a new area and the opportunity for mistakes, he's higher even among experienced employees.

The next one is about having a policy document for using chat, GPT and other such tools and the associated confidentiality and privacy challenges. This is very important because once a policy is there, employees can refer. And have their queries addressed. In the absence of a documented policy. There is the risk of assumptions being made. We should make every effort to avoid such mishaps. So have a clear, documented policy which can be accessed by employees whenever they have questions or doubts. Okay. All the actions that I've covered so far are applicable to your vendor organizations as well, because we all use vendors. So all the actions that I mentioned apply equally to our vendors. Ensure the vendors are adequately sensitized, trained and monitored. The growth of Chatgpt is very similar to the growth we saw when the Internet became popular. So don't take these private privacy and confidentiality issues associated with Chatgpt and other such tools lightly.

Beat Privacy Issues | Create a Custom ChatGPT like App

In this chapter we are going to create our own ChatGPT like chatbot. In fact, this chatbot is going to use ChatGPT but in the background. We are going to use Streamlit, which is a framework to create and deploy machine learning applications as a web application. You may ask, is this really needed? After all, we have ChatGPT. The issue we are trying to address is data privacy. When you prompt your query in ChatGPT, that prompt forms part of their future training data. Always remember this. So it makes sense to have your own chat bot that your employees can use without fear of data privacy issues.

Here we are trying to create a web application that can write blogs for us. So we need to get an API key from OpenAI. That key will be used in our Python program. So how do we get an API key? We go to openai.com. We click login and sign in using our email ID. Once we log in we see three options. Click API. Now choose your account at the top right corner. Click view API keys. You can create the key using the Create new Secret key option. You can copy that key and use it. I have blackened the keys for security purposes. I'm going to cover some coding software in this chapter. I'm doing that to explain the choices. We have to fine tune the model.

That is, we can change the characteristics of the model output marginally. We are doing this fine tuning so that we can direct the model to deliver the output in a particular fashion. We first start by importing the necessary libraries. We will paste the key that we copied earlier in this particular block of code. Let us define the main function that will run the Streamlined application. We have three options. First is blog topic generation. Next is blogchapter generation and finally blog content generation. Blog topics prompt defines a function to generate blog topics using OpenAI. OpenAI dot completion dot create sends a request to OpenAI to generate text based on prompt written response dot choices. Returns the generated text. Finally let us see the options to tune the model. I've highlighted the parameters that can be tuned.

Tuning influences the behavior and performance of text generation models. Max tokens controls the maximum number of tokens in the generated text. A lower value may result in more concise text, while a higher value may produce more verbose text. Top P refers to the cumulative probability cut off for sampling the next token. A lower value, like 0.1 means only the top 10% most probable tokens are considered, while a value of 0.9 includes 90% of the token probability mass. Frequency penalty penalizes tokens that are generated frequently, which can help reduce repetition. Presence penalty penalizes new tokens that haven't appeared before, which can encourage the model to reuse existing tokens. I used the word token a few times before. What is this token? Token is nothing but the word that has been generated.

The choice of the engine will affect how the model generates text based on the prompt. The temperature parameter in the context of neural network based text generation, such as ChatGPT, controls the randomness of the output generated by the model. It is a hyper parameter that affects the probability distribution over the tokens. When sampling the mixed token in a sequence, a lower temperature value such as 0.120.5 makes the model's output more deterministic, meaning the model is more likely to pick the most probable word at each step, resulting in more focused and coherent text. A temperature value of one means no scaling is applied, and the original logits are used for sampling.

This generates a balance between randomness and determinism. A higher temperature value, such as 1.5 to 2, makes the model's output more random, meaning the model is more likely to pick less probable words, resulting in more creative but potentially less coherent or sensible text in the given code. We have used a temperature of 0.7. It means the output will lean towards being more focused and deterministic compared to a temperature of, say, one, but with a slight level of randomness to potentially generate more creative or varied text. I'm ready to execute this py file. I will execute the file from the Anaconda prompt. Let's go to the start menu. Choose Anaconda prompt. Let's open this. We will first change the directory reference CD desktop. Chris Tremlett.

The file is stored in the Streamlit folder that is there in my desktop, which is why I did this. Let us execute the code Streamlite run app is the dot. Py is the name of the file and click enter. The file has been executed and we have the application in front of us. So these are the three options: I can create a topic , I can create a chapter, I can create content, I can input my query and I can generate a blog without any worry of data privacy issues. Now let us see if the tool is working well. We will prompt you to generate a blog topic on data science with Python. Let's click send or Enter and see if it generates the blog topic. Yes, it has been generated. Let's press send once again and see if it generates another blog topic. It is generated this time the top five libraries for data science. We created a blog topic earlier.

Now let us create a blog chapter. My prompt is how to use pandas for data analysis, and I want blog chapters to be created in the drop down menu. I've chosen a chapter, so let's click enter and see the response. Yes, it is generated. If you see, I did not use the words blockchapter in my prompt. Blockchapter has been generated based on the choice I made in the dropdown menu. A little earlier, while discussing the code for the Streamlined application, I mentioned the parameters that can be changed. When I say we can change the parameter, I am referring to the tuning process. You can change the temperature and other parameters depending on the kind of output you want. That kind of flexibility, that level of flexibility, is there only when you go for a custom application.

Beat Privacy Issues | Chat with your PDF document

In this chapter, we are going to see yet another interesting use case. How about uploading a PDF document and chatting with the document? How cool, right? All this while using chat. GPT is the latest technology. Since we will take the route of using OpenAI's API key, we don't need to worry about the data privacy issues. Here we are merely accessing the chat GPT model data to remain fairly safe. We start by importing the necessary chapters. We save this file as a.py file and then execute it from the Anaconda Command prompt. Let's do that and go through the working of this chatbot. Let us access the Anaconda command prompt from the windows startup menu. Let's click this. We will first change the directory reference and then execute the file.

CD desktop. And then see the Streamlite. The. The. the.py file is there in the Streamlit folder, which is there in my desktop, which is why I made this directory reference change. Now let us run the file. Streamlit run. PDF chat bot.py. That's the name of the file. Let's click enter. Yep. The file has been executed. Let's go through the working of the app by accessing the IP address that we have got here. Let us upload a file. This is a file about Net Promoter Score. Net Promoter Score is a wonderful concept in the area of customer loyalty and customer experience. Instead of asking whether you are satisfied with a product or service, ask whether you will refer to your friends and family. The difference in the percentage of detractors and promoters is the NPS score.

Wonderful concept that is strongly correlated with profitability and revenue. The file is uploaded and the details of the files have been extracted in this area. Now let us start asking the question. I want to start off by asking who are the. Authors of the document. Let's click submit and see the response. Yes, it is responded correctly. Now let us ask one more question. My next question is what methodological? Concerns that are being raised in this document. Let's correct the spelling mistake and click submit. Okay. It indicates the methodological concerns that have been raised in the document. So you can create a similar app for your business needs and leverage the knowledge repository of your organization.

Where should a CxO focus?

If you are a decision maker in your organization, where should you focus with respect to? Generative model like ChatGPT? That's what we are going to look at in this chapter. In the world of software, there is the perennial debate between buy versus build. Should you build your own software or buy a pre-built one? There are pros and cons with each decision. The same debate is applicable in the world of ChatGPT. And other generative models like Google Bard. You see the immense potential with ChatGPT. So should you build one like that or use a pre-built model? There are multiple factors to consider when building your own version of ChatGPT or Google Bard.

Developing your own model requires a team of experts with deep knowledge in machine learning, natural language processing, or NLP and software engineering. It requires a significant amount of high quality training data. Building an AI model from scratch is a resource intensive process. AI models aren't set and forget solutions. They require regular maintenance and fine tuning. And you would need to implement practices to ensure the model's use cases align with privacy laws and are fair and unbiased. Given these considerations, leveraging an existing API like Openai's, ChatGPT or Google's bot might be a more practical option.

This approach allows you to benefit from the state of the art technology without having to worry about the challenges of developing and maintaining your own model. You can focus on integrating and using the API or application programming interface to achieve your business goals. However, there might be specific scenarios where building your own model is justified. For example, if you have unique requirements that are not addressed by existing APIs or if you have the necessary expertise and resources and see strategic value in owning and controlling your own technology. In such situations, having your own model is definitely justified.

Let us also keep in mind that there are some middle ground solutions that exist between developing an AI model from scratch and using an off the shelf API. Though these are very early days, some providers offer APIs that allow you to fine tune Pre-trained models on your specific tasks. For example, you could take a Pre-trained language model like GPT three or GPT four and fine tune it on your specific dataset. This way you get a model that is tailored to your needs without having to train it from scratch. Similar to model fine tuning in transfer learning. You start with a pre-trained model and then retrain it on a smaller dataset specific to your needs.

This requires some model training expertise, but much less than building a model from scratch. Some companies provide custom solutions tailored to your specific needs. These companies build, train and maintain the models for you, but the models are specifically designed for your use case. Remember that while these solutions provide a balance between customization and ease of use, they still require some level of expertise, resources for implementation and maintenance and a strong understanding of your data and use case. So if you are a CXO of a large company, what should you do? You can definitely invest in infrastructure. As a large corporation, it is crucial to have the necessary infrastructure in place to accommodate operations.

This includes both hardware for data processing and software to execute algorithms. You can also build an in-house team of professionals like data scientists and machine learning engineers who can drive your initiatives. Not everyone in your company needs to be an expert, but it is beneficial for your workforce to be literate. So consider setting up training programs to build familiarity across departments. You can also integrate AI into your business strategy, and this is a no brainer. So identify key areas where AI can provide value and set clear goals to measure its success. Remember that usage should be ethical, transparent and responsible.

So establish policies to ensure data privacy and fairness in AI models. Now, if you are a CXO in a mid-sized company, where should you focus with respect to generative AI? So start by identifying opportunities. This must be your focus area for you. Understand where I can bring value to your business. This might be to streamline processes, improve customer service, or offer innovative products. Instead of building in-house capabilities, it might be more feasible to partner with external vendors who specialize in AI. You can also experiment with pilot projects. Start small with AI projects, learn from them, and then scale up.

This minimizes risk and allows you to provide value before significant investment. Ensure that you have a good data strategy, and rely on good quality data. Organize and manage your data well to effectively train AI models. Last but not the least, promote a culture of innovation. So foster a workplace culture that is open to experimenting with AI and other emerging technologies. Now let's look at the small company, and if you are a CXO, what should you do? I will suggest that you leverage AI as a service, take advantage of cloud based solutions which allow you to reap the benefits of AI without significant investment in infrastructure. Focus on immediate benefits. Implement AI in areas that can show immediate value, such as customer service, chat bots or automation of repetitive tasks.

You can also build partnerships that form strategic partnerships with companies or even academic institutions. They can provide you with access to advanced resources or expertise. An important factor is staying updated with trends. As a small company, staying agile and up to date with the latest trends in AI can definitely provide a competitive edge. The last point is about ensuring data security regardless of the size of your company and the size of your implementation. It is important to handle data responsibly. Implement proper data security measures to protect your business and also customers. So keep these points. Keep these perspectives in mind as you go about exploring generative tools and models.

Google Bard: A Worthy Competitor to ChatGPT

Barred from Google is a worthy competitor to ChatGPT and it comes with a variety of features. It is also a generative AI tool like ChatGPT. Google has recently introduced some functionalities. Notable among them is the introduction of Google Lens features. That is, you can even upload an image using the plus sign here and Googlebot will read the contents of that image and convert that image into text. It can even convert that image that is the contents of the image into a table. And we can take that table into Google worksheet for further analysis. In my opinion, this single feature is a breakthrough one and it can disrupt the automation and OCR markets in a big way. Let us try that out. So you understand what I am talking about.

We will start by uploading the file. Currently you can upload Jpeg, PNG and web web format images. This web format is something that is unique to Google. We are going to upload either a Jpeg or a PNG file and we will demonstrate the capabilities. So let us upload the image file by clicking this. So we will click the upload file. I'm going to upload this particular file. It contains details of the extent of spam calls in different countries. It comes from truecaller, which is. A well known app for detecting spam calls. So the prompt I'm going to give is can you convert? The contents. Of the below image. Into a table. Very simple one. Okay. And let's click submit and see what we get. While we are waiting for Bart to complete, let's look at the image.

As I said, this image represents the extent of spam calls in 2021 across different countries. The information is available in the form of a. The graphical visual. And as I said, it comes from Truecaller. Brazil tops the list, followed by Peru, Ukraine, India and many other countries. The US is actually in the 20th spot with a performance of less than five scam calls per user per month. Okay, so let's go back to the results of Bart. It is able to extract information from Bart. Okay. The output is in the form of a table. So which is the important one? Now let's come to the most important one. I can export this into Google sheets.

So this entire information can be exported in the form of a worksheet. And for this we will use Google sheets. So let's click export to sheet. This information is getting exported. It's ready. Let's click Open sheets. It opens up in a new browser and you can see the information in the form of a worksheet. We can use this worksheet to do different types of analysis. As I said, this is very, very useful information that all of us can explore. There are other functionalities in Googlebot that are worth noting. You can export this to other people. You can share this as a draft in Gmail. You can Of course export it to docs.

That is Google's equivalent for Microsoft Word or you can share it. Let's click share. You can share this particular image, this particular table. You can add the contents. You can even get a public link. Let me demonstrate other features in

Googlebot. The prompt I'm going to use is what is the outlook for generative AI? In the next five years. Provide the response. In bullet points format. Okay, let's click Submit. We now have the response from Bart. If you want, you can ask for the response in a more professional, simpler or shorter format. You come here and click this. You can change the kind of response you want here. I want a simpler response. Let me click this and we will get a simplified version of the response from Google. But compared to the earlier version, this one is simpler.

You can look at other drafts as well. Okay. You can check the draft too. It is different. Draft three is also different from draft one and draft two. Let's go back to draft one. We can ask Bart to read the response to us. You just have to click listen and Bart will read the response to you. Okay. Bart is available in multiple languages like Spanish and Hindi. Now let's ask Bart to translate the above into Spanish and Hindi. Translate the above into Spanish and Hindi. And let's click submit and see what we get. Bard is able to provide the response in Spanish and Hindi as well. Now, if you click listen, Bard will read out the response in Spanish and in Hindi. This is very useful, right? Now I want to do some data analysis. I have a dataset that is stored in GitHub.

It pertains to a banking scenario where an applicant's income and other details are analyzed before a decision is made whether to give the loan or not. I want Googlebot to analyze the data and provide some insights. I'm just going to provide the link. So let's go to the bar and provide the necessary prompt. So the prompt is can you analyze? The data. Stored in GitHub and I'm giving the link. Let's click and see the results. It says I'm a text based AI and that's outside of my capabilities. It is unable to analyze the data stored in. A public database like GitHub. So what I'm going to do is copy the data and paste the data in the prompt area itself and ask Google to analyze. Let's see if we are successful. Analyze the below data. I'm just copy pasting parts of the data from the data that is available in the GitHub link.

And let's click Enter, see if Google is able to analyze the trends, at least indicate the names of the columns. I think Google has analyzed it, has identified the column names, it has identified the averages, and it's also giving insights. That's good, right? The average loan amount is this. The average term majority of the borrowers are married, 63% majority have a high school diploma, 78%. Very good insights about the data. It also indicates what are the additional insights that can be gained from the data. It talks about correlation between two variables. That is a positive correlation between income and loan negative correlation. All these insights can be made use of this very, very good analysis. So Google is able to do a very good job in analyzing data. The only problem seems to be in accessing data stored in different databases. I'm sure that Google will address this limitation in the coming version of Google Bar.

What is Prompt Engineering

In earlier chapters I mentioned prompt engineering. This term prompt engineering has gained prominence in recent times. Have you heard this term before? Well, prompt engineering is nothing but the art and science of asking questions. Questions elicit answers. Different questions will yield different answers. Some people are good at asking questions, while others miss the opportunity to extract information. The process of engaging with ChatGPT can be greatly enhanced by understanding prompt engineering. These techniques are applicable even when you engage with a human being. Prompt engineering is all about being specific.

If your question is vague, the other party may not understand you well. This is true even for an expert. The next important point is about choice of words. Sometimes we write. Choice of words can go a long way in communicating the message succinctly. To assess a project, I can ask how the project is going on? I may get a response like it is moving along well. On the other hand, if I ask when are we going to complete the project as compared to the agreed completion date? I can expect a much better and specific response. The next one is context. Context is very important as it helps to understand the background. Without context, the expert or an expert system like ChatGPT cannot understand or appreciate why the question is being asked.

Context can make a big difference in the quality and specificity of responses. Sometimes we have to reframe. That is, change the way we ask questions. Instead of saying you never listen to me and it is ruining and it is ruining our relationship. I could say I feel unheard and it is causing me pain. Last but not the least, patience. Even an expert system like ChatGPT will not give you the kind of response you are expecting immediately. You have to be patient. Change your approach to reframing role play and other ideas. It is just like talking to an expert friend. He or she knows a lot of things, but may not be able to respond the way we want immediately. So be patient while engaging with ChatGPT and change your approach. If you don't get a satisfactory response in the first instance, that is prompt engineering for you.

RPA

While Industry 4.0 is about industrial automation, RPA is about office automation. By that I mean automation of mundane, repetitive, rule-based tasks that are done in front of the computer. RPA is essentially a computer software that resides inside a computer or a laptop. It imitates human actions. Done in front of the computer. So please note that. Because RPA involves automation of mundane, repetitive tasks, your processes or tasks need to be standardized. If the process is not standardized, it becomes difficult to automate the task or the process because repetitive tasks are prone to errors. By automating such repetitive tasks, we reduce the errors in a big way.

OK, we can even bring down the errors to nearly zero. And the productivity of the process also improved significantly because this is done by the mission. Right. So RPA is an entity that imitates or mimics human actions. Right. It can be an automation of a task or a broader end to end process. OK, you cannot do task automation and. Workflow automation also. We are going to see that shortly, but essentially we are talking of automating repetitive rule based tasks, right. And these tasks are automatically done by the RPA software. Let us not forget that repetitive tasks invariably involve errors when done by human beings. So implementing a RPA solution in a process will result in almost zero errors, thereby leading to higher productivity and lower costs.

That's a big advantage, right? OK, what are some of the examples of RPA? extracting information from images and documents Let's say you have an invoice you want to extract, purchase order number that can be done by using RPA. If you want to prepare reports and send it to multiple people as part of a distribution, RPA is very helpful. you want to process some steps like payment to vendors that can also be done by RPA software, sending updates, monitoring systems, database administrator activities, rule-based decision making. Can all be done by RPA software. Please note that all these tasks need to be standardized before you attempt automation and RPA exercise in a non standardized process is invariably going to be a failure. OK. The question that is often asked in the world of RPA is RPA really AI.

RPA at its core involves mimicking human actions done in front of the computer, whereas machine learning artificial intelligence is about mimicking human thought process in machine learning the systems enhance or improvise on their own over a period of time. In fact, the accuracy of machine learning applications improves over time. The applications learn from their own mistakes. That doesn't happen in RPA, because RPA is about a rule based system. So please keep this in mind. So RPA is strictly not an AI. However, RPA is increasingly using machine learning technologies to address some of the challenges in automation, especially the challenges in non standardized processes. So please keep this in mind. OK. Chatbot or virtual assistance is also an example of RPA.

Chatbot is also a computer software that resides in the applications of the organization. Whenever you have a query about a product or service, you may want to engage with them. Organization. So instead of engaging with a real life human being, you engage with a digital assistant, the digital assistant would have collected the frequently asked questions of customers and prepared the list of responses to such questions. If your questions or query falls within the frequently asked questions, the chat bot will provide the necessary response. If your question is outside that list, it will invariably ask you for your phone number or email I.D. so that someone from the organization can contact you. So you see, chatbot is a rule based RPA software.

However, this RPA software is increasingly using deep learning and machine learning technologies, in particular technology called natural language processing to make the interaction between virtual assistants and customers a lot smoother and a lot more human. OK, you will also see the chat window pop up in e-commerce sites. So when you're trying to buy a product or service, you will see a pop up window. A Pop-Up window for engaging with the company's virtual assistants so that your credit can be addressed by the virtual assistant and you end up buying their products or services. Right. So Chatbot is essentially RPA. However, it is using AI technologies. To improve customer satisfaction and to resolve customer queries.

Intelligent Automation

In the previous chapter, we learned about RPA. Now, let's see intelligent automation, which builds on the RPA. If you really see it's all about automation of rule-based, repetitive and simple tasks. Many of the processes involved complex tasks which require an enhanced version of RPA, called intelligent automation. So intelligent automation makes use of A.I. and OCR technologies to automate such complex tasks and tasks that require cognitive abilities. OCR is optical character recognition. OCR helps us to retrieve specific information from images and scanned documents like hospital records and purchase orders. See, you can extract a purchase order number from an invoice using OCR and then you can do any kind of processing. OK, that is the benefit with advancement in OCR. NLP if you see. It's a wonderful technology that is making virtual assistance more human.

NLP is the intersection of three disciplines, computing, AI and human languages. NLP has helped chat boxes to move away from frequently asked questions to cover more possibilities. NLP is actually at the forefront of conversational systems like Alexa. You can have Alexa, like applications for your prostheses, OK? That is the biggest benefit of advancements in NLP, okay. So intelligent automation addresses the challenges faced in real life scenarios like multiple formats, standardization issues, unstructured data. I would like to highlight here that intelligent automation involves moving away from template or tool based solutions. What I mean by this is that it is possible to develop. A grounds of automation solution, much like a ground software project to address your process requirements, unique challenges such a solution will meet your automation requirements much better than a tool based solution. And this includes a higher ROI too. It is the power of intelligent automation for you.

Task Vs Workflow Automation

Should you automate a task? or should you automate a workflow? is an important question. That you need to ask yourself when it comes to automation. The example of your seeing it on screen. Is actually an automation of an end to end process. Workflow automation involves the payment process. Specific information. Is extracted from purchase order, invoice and goods receipt order not documents, such information is then fed into SAP for triggering payment to vendors instead of automating the entire workflow. You can also automate the specific tasks in this end to end process like entering information. In SAP or extracting information from purchase order.

The advantage with workflow automation is that you can realize headcount reduction, it is not always possible in task automation. Task automation no doubt reduces errors and improves productivity, but headcount reduction, which leads to cost reduction, doesn't always happen. Please keep this in mind. Start with task automation, but your aim should be to move to workflow or end to end process automation. It is only in a workflow or encrypted process automation that you can realize headcount savings leading to cost reduction. So please keep that in your mind.

Case Study 8: Intelligent Automation

So having seen what RPA is, I want to show you a case study, right? It's something we did in a large organization. What you see on the screen is really an invoice. As I said, one of the many repetitive activities that people in organizations do is copy information from one fine. Right. And they take it from one system. And then whatever they have extracted, they go and copy it in another system, which is then taken apart for the processing. That's what is happening right to Details in this invoice. material code , net amount. the P thirty nine eight two one two one four seven eight four. This has to be copied into another application. It comes as a scanned document previously before we implemented the RPA solution. Someone used to see it right.

Sometimes a printout or sometimes a scan copy in a computer will look for material, code and net amt fields, then look for values. Right. There's no way to copy, so that person will see, read and then go and enter that value in another system for further processing. Totally manual, right? He will read P thirty nine, eight two one two then go and type P, thirty nine, eight two one two. Net amount. is one four seven eight four point zero zero. The person will actually read it then go and enter into another application, a totally manual process. As I said, this is how many organizations still work. And what we did is we tried to automate this process because this was coming as a scanned to document the system, can actually pick it up, can pick up and go and update in another system. But there are challenges.

If you see in this case, in this format, the value of the material code appears in the same line. Whereas in another invoice, the value appears one row below. The net amount is also the same case, it appears one row below and here it appears in the same. Right. So this is not repetitive, but some element of variation, is there? So we had to. Adopt the RPA solution to address this variation in input. It's a challenge which we were able to overcome. So we created an application, which is what you see, right? This is the place where you upload the document, you enter the name of the field here, and you also mention where the value of that field lies in that document, is it in the same line.? is it, just below our how many rows below.? Right, see here, this is just below or it could be in the second line or it could be in the third line or it could be the fourth line.

See, this level of detail is needed in RPA solutions, but not so much in an AI or ML solution. So all these details are mentioned, you upload the file, you enter the name of the field here, and then you mention where the field value is mentioned in the document. And then you click submit the values extract. Right, can you see here. Sample is there. Then you enter the field value and you say that it is in the same line, the next one is net amount, you say that it is just below the field name, right? How many rows below? This is one row below. and then you click submit. As you can see, the details are being extracted. You can then download.

or you can, whatever you have downloaded or whatever you have extracted, you can then go and upload in another system. Right here, you copied this in an Excel file, which can then be used to upload in other systems. So that's really the benefit of the RPA solution. What was done manually is now automated. The repetitive, mundane tasks need not be done by employees. The employee's time is free so they can go and work in more value-adding activities. In fact, the one that you see here is part of an end to end process automation. The example that you saw in the invoice. The RPA, RPA application extracts the value of the fields from the invoice, it updates an excel.

And as I said, it gets updated into SAP which is an ERP system, the entire sequence here we are talking of an end to end process. All that the employees have to do is scan the document and put it in a folder, that's all. what is called an invoice folder. That's all they have to do, all the other activities, the process of extracting the field value, updating an excel. In some cases, this may not even be needed after you've extracted, you go and update into SAP. For further processing, the entire activity is now automated. Previously, this was manually done. Somebody will extract and then somebody will go and update in a system so two different people do it, two separate sets of activities. Now, this process is automated. The end to end process is automated, it results in faster processing.

As I said, productivity is enhanced. People's time is free . The employees were doing the data entry or seeing the document, reading the value, all those activities were happening. Now,

It is no longer needed. The automation solution is able to automate fairly end to end processes. That's the power of. RPA Do you understand? Are you able to appreciate now what RPA can do and as I said, RPA is now leveraging the power of machine learning. The kind of solutions we are going to see in future will be. Will be very sophisticated with the two technologies coming together. In solving automation problems.

Challenges in AI and RPA deployments

Before we conclude, I want to highlight the challenges in AI and RPA deployments. After all, to be prepared is after victory. In the case of machine learning and deep learning, data availability is a big challenge. If you remember, I shared this as part of the fraud detection case study. Do you really think organizations are ready with all the necessary data? The answer is a big no, even if you have data, past references to the objectives in this case, past references to fraud. And the corresponding data for all these factors may not be available. That is also a challenge. Many times we have to make do with whatever is available. Sometimes it can take even up to a year to have the minimum set of data. Please note that machine learning and deep learning applications require a large volume of data.

If you have only limited data, your predictability takes a hit. So it's a delicate balance between data availability and predictability or accuracy. That is why sponsorship from management is very critical. When it comes to RPA, two things are rather important. There are two main challenges. One is whether you should go for task automation or workflow automation. Go for workflow automation, if kept on cost reduction are your primary objectives. When you automate the tasks, you can possibly save only a small portion of the process operator's time. corresponding to the time taken to do that particular task. This will not save headcount. please keep this in mind. The other is all the process documentation. Do you think this level of process documentation is sufficient? The answer Is a big no.

We need granular level details like the specific field name to be extracted from a document and the field name of the application where this information needs to be entered into. Business analysts have never done these kinds of documentation. In many cases, the granular level of details is intuitive to the process operator. So even if you sit for a process documentation exercise, with the process operator, the operator may not mention the minutest details because the minutest details are so intuitive. There is Process mining software available that makes this documentation exercise a little easier. But business analysts need to do double the work to document the process to the level that is fit for automation.

What is AutoML

In this training program so far, we have covered artificial intelligence, machine learning, natural language processing and robotic process automation. We have also called the technologies that are driving the rise of AI and the technologies, enabling the rise of A.I.. In addition to that, we have covered eight case studies, so you get a clear idea of where to apply this wonderful technology in your line of business. Now I'm going to cover your recent trend in the world of AI. It is known as Auto ML. Auto ML is all about developing and deploying machine learning and other advanced A.I. models without writing. A single line of code. For the purpose of demonstrating auto ML, I will be using it. Google Cloud's vertex AI platform. vertex AI is the no code auto ML platform from Google Cloud.

I'm going to be demonstrating how to develop and deploy the churned prediction model. Using Vertex platform. For you to understand how to develop and deploy. The machine learning model, you must know some additional concepts related to machine learning like. What is the dependent variable? What is an independent variable? What are the characteristics of the classification versus the regression problem? How will you assess the accuracy of a classification model versus the regression model? So we will first cover these concepts and then get into. Developing and deploying the churn prediction model in Google Cloud Vertex AI platform. And in this particular chapter. Let us understand the evolution of auto ML.

The IT industry has been at the forefront of automating business processes and activities in organization, the automation done by I.T. industry for other industries. Spilled over to the IT industry itself. Twenty years ago, to develop an application, we used to write about ten thousand or twenty thousand lines of code. Today, it is possible to develop similar applications with just a few hundred lines of code. This code heavy to low-code evolution has now become a no-code development environment, where we can develop applications without writing a single line of code. So this automation in the IT industry has now come to the world of machine learning and deep learning also. So automation is everywhere. In this program.

You're going to see how to develop and deploy machine learning and deep learning models without writing a single line of code. The example that you see on the screen is a case of multiple linear regression in an insurance industry. We are trying to predict how much the insurance company should charge a customer by considering these six independent variables like age, sex, BMI, region, etc.. Without auto ML, it takes a lot of effort to develop and deploy the models. By using Vertex AI, that is Google Cloud's Auto ML platform, I will be able to develop and deploy this model fairly easily. All I need to do is upload the dataset, indicating whether it's a case of classification or regression problem. What is classification versus regression? we're going to see in detail in a subsequent chapter. I'm going to choose the objective and then indicate the target variable.

That is the dependent variable. That is what we're trying to predict. We're trying to predict charges, right? So I need to select charges. That's all. After that, it's a question of a few clicks. Your model is ready. Your few more clicks. The model is deployed. That's how easy it is to use and apply auto ML for your line of business. Hope you understand what auto ML is. This is the latest trend in the world of IT industry and in the world of machine learning. Deep learning too.

Introduction to Google Cloud's Vertex AI

Welcome to vertex AI Google Cloud's Auto ML platform. vertex offers prediction for four different scenarios. The tabular one for classification/regression and forecasting. For text prediction that is using NLP. It offers four different types of prediction services: single label or multi label classification, sentiment analysis and even entity extraction from documents. What I really like about this AutoML platform is it offers predictions even for images and chapters, right? So you can do single label or multi label image classification. You can identify objects and you can segment images also. In chapter, you can identify specific actions, you can track objects and you can classify the chapters also. Isn't it wonderful that Google Cloud offers so many options for us? And we can do all these kinds of predictions without writing a single line of code. OK.

Very intuitive, very user friendly. That's what I found, vertex AI to be, and that's what you're going to experience in the subsequent chapters. There are. Other aspects related to vertex AI for deploying the model, using endpoints or batch predictions. OK, we're going to see all of that in subsequent chapters. OK, so how do you access vertex AI? You come to console.cloud.google.com/vertexAI. That is to get started. OK. First, you need to register using your email I.D. and you need to provide your credit card details to get started. Google, Of course, provides free credit during your trial period. But even for that, you'll need to provide your credit card details. I strongly encourage you to try it.

The other thing that I liked about Vertex is that there is quite a bit of documentation and use cases also covered here. OK? You can explore all of them in vertex AI. In some areas you will see this suffix preview. It means that this particular feature is not fully ready. OK. Some parts of the feature are under testing. Under development. OK. If you don't see the suffix preview, it means it is completely available. OK, all the features are ready to be used. OK. Let's get started.

Dependent Vs Independent Variable

This chapter is about understanding the concept of dependent vs independent variables. This is a very important concept. Now, let's see this. with an example. The height to which a plant grows is dependent on. The amount of water that is used and the quantity of fertilizers. There are other factors like the day on which the seeds were planted, weather, and so many other factors. But let's just look at two factors: the height to which a plant grows and the two factors you are analyzing are water and fertilizers. If you see the height. OK. As a factor, or as a variable, is dependent on fertilizer and water. OK, so the growth of the plant is dependent on these two.

While fertilizers and water are not dependent on anything, they are dependent on something. About which we are not concerned as of now. so we are considering the height of the plant. And the height of the plant is dependent on fertilizers and water. So in this case. Quantity of fertilizers and quantity of water are independent variables, and the height of the plant is a dependent variable. Do you understand this concept? You have to establish these dependent and independent variables at the start of your machine learning or deep learning project. So this is a very, very important concept. Right now, let's see some examples from Real World.

The insurance company is trying to ascertain how much they should charge the customer for insurance, right? So the factors they will consider are age, sex, BMI, BMI is body mass index, number of children the person has got, whether he is a smoker or not. Which region he or she comes from? Right. So all these are independent variables and insurance charges are my dependent variable. That means the quantum of insurance charges is dependent on these factors. Are you getting it? are dependent on these factors. Let's see one more example from the world of banking. The bank is trying to ascertain whether loans should be granted or not. OK.

And what are the factors? The bank is taking into account gender, whether that individual is married or not, number of dependents, education, whether that individual is self-employed or working for an organization. What is the applicant's income? Is there a co applicant income? What is the loan amount? loan tenure, credit history and property area? If you see there are 11 factors right. And all these 11 factors are independent variables. And why should loan be granted or not is a dependent variable, because should loan be granted or not is dependent on all these factors? Right? It is like why is a function of X one x two and so on and so forth? Right. I hope you're all clear about the concept of dependent on independent variables.

Regression and Classification Concepts

In this chapter, we will understand regression and classification concepts a bit more in detail. We introduce these concepts in the earlier chapter. Let's get started with an example. The example I'm considering. A student studies for a certain number of hours, and he gets different kinds of marks. we're trying to establish a correlation between the number of hours studied and the marks obtained. I'm going to use Excel to create the scatterplot. OK. This can be created using Python or here as well or any programming language, for that matter. If you see this we use a scatter plot. A scatterplot is used in regression, and it shows the extent of the relationship between X and Y.

What is the dependent variable And independent variable in this case? Marks obtained are the dependent variable and number of hours studied is the independent variable, because marks obtained are dependent on the number of hours studied, right? And the number of hours studied is not dependent on anything. Maybe it's dependent on something about which we are not concerned for now. OK, we are interested in establishing the relationship between the number of hours studied and marks obtained. OK, so how will you go about creating this in excel? So you first select the data points and you come to insert and then click the option here, OK, and then you will click this scatterplot, OK, and you will have a graph like this, right? So that is the starting point for you here.

The relationship between the two is linear. OK. It is not logarithmic or anything else. So what is logarithmic? We are going to see that shortly. That means when I say that the relationship is linear, it means I can show this relationship in the form of a straight line, right? So that is known as a linear relationship. OK. I can show the relationship between my dependent variable and independent variable in the form of a straight line. And what is the straight line that I am talking about? I am going to fit a line that will cover all these data points. In fact, that line is known as goodness of fit. Right. So let's create that goodness of fit. How will I do it? I first have to select these data points, just click one of the data points, OK and right click. You can see these options will be there. Click Add Trend Line.

And you will have this straight line come up, and you also choose to display the equation on the chart. OK. You can also choose Display R-Squared, remember. We covered R square in the previous chapter. So I display the equation. So this equation shows the relationship between dependent variable and independent variable. If you recollect your mathematics days this equation looks like mx+c, y equals mx+c. That means the number of marks obtained equals 10.862 into the number of hours studied, plus 41.901 Right. If, let's say a student comes, you know, that particular student comes and tells you that he has studied for 1.25 hours. All I need to do is put 1.25 here. That is 10.862 into 1.25 plus

41.901 will give the marks the student will get when he or she studies for 1.25.

hours, right? So I have not only established the Fit, I can also predict the future. Right. Are you getting it? So what is this Y equals mx+c? M is known as gradient, and C is known as the intercept. This intercept corresponds to the value where the line meets the y axis. OK. And slope is nothing but this distance divided by this distance. It is also known as Delta Y, divided by Delta X. In this case, this distance is four and this distance is two. Four. Divided by two is two. I can also draw a smaller triangle and the same height divided by base that will give the same value of M. OK. I can draw a smaller triangle or a slightly bigger triangle also. OK, wherever you draw a triangle on this line and when you compute the height divided by base, the value of M that you get will be the same. Right.

Are you understanding linear regression? OK. number of hours studied and Marks obtained OK in this case. The line meets the y axis at minus four, so intercept is minus four and gradient is? see I have drawn a smaller triangle, I didn't draw a bigger triangle like this. and the same height divided by base two, divided by one. Will you know my slope or gradient? And I can have more than one variable also right in the example that I just share a number of hours studied is one independent variable. And in the case of multiple linear regression, you will have more than one independent variable. Please note that the dependent variable will always be only one. Right? So here I am looking at two variables, right? In the case of multiple linear regression. I'm trying to predict what will be the quantum of carbon dioxide emission in a vehicle. And I am predicting that using two independent variables: volume of the vehicle and weight of the vehicle. Right.

So this is a case of multiple linear regression. Right. I don't have just one factor, but I have more than one factor. And here also the relationship is linear. That means I can express this in the form of a straight line. Right now, let's see. Logistic regression. OK, let's understand that with an example. Here we are trying to predict the malignancy of a tumor, what is malignancy, that means whether the tumor is really cancerous or not, malignancy means cancer. I am trying to predict malignancy based on tumor size. I have plotted instances of tumor size and the malignancy here, OK? And I have represented it in the form of a graph.

If I tried to fit a linear relationship in this, which is a straight line, I cannot fit all the points, right? As you can see here. If I tried to fit a straight line like this, even if I move that line, you know a bit to the left, these points will be left out. Right. So my fit is not good at all. A straight line cannot cover all the data points. If you recollect the linear regression, the straight line covered almost all the data points, right? That means the fit is good. Here, The foot is so bad that you cannot have a linear regression. You need what is known as logistic regression, because when it is in the form of a curve like this, it covers all the data points. Right. Are you understanding? here. Because I have a curve, it covers all the data points with almost all the data points .

And in the case of a linear model, I have what is known as Y equals mx+c or B not plus b one xbox one is the slope and B not is the intercept. In the case of logistic regression, we use what is known as sigmoid function, OK, which is nothing but one plus e to the power of minus B not plus b one x this e to The power of minus is basically a way of writing logarithmic value, right? And the output is in the case of linear regression. The output is the numeric value in the case of a logistic regression or a logic model. The output is a probability right. That is whether the tumor is cancerous or not. It'll have a value between zero and one. Do you understand the difference between a linear relationship and a Logistic relationship? OK.

Let's see an example where we compare linear and logistic using similar or same independent variables? OK, let's take the carbon dioxide emission. I'm using these two x one x two vehicle volume and vehicle weight. That's my independent variables. I'm trying to predict the quantum of carbon dioxide emission. I use multiple linear regression if I predict what is the likelihood of carbon dioxide emission coming from that vehicle. I use logistic regression. Please note here I'm using the word likelihood that means it is a probability, which means it can either value between zero and one. Are you getting it? In logistic regression, one more aspect is because the dependent variable has a value between zero and one, your X1 and X2 should also have a value between zero and one.

Right. But you see here the values here are not between zero and one, right? They are numeric values, so I need to convert the numeric into. Logarithmic value. And then I will apply logistic regression. I would like to add here that logistic regression is actually a classification algorithm because the outcome will be. Yes or no, right? True or false? In this case, the likelihood of carbon dioxide emission will be high or low, right? It won't be a numerical value, which will be the case in regression. So in regression.

The output will be in numeric value in the classification algorithm. The output will be yes, no, good, bad, true, false, zero or one kind of output. Right? though we use the word regression in logistic regression? It is actually a classification algorithm. That's one point. The other point is logistic regression actually belongs to a group of models known as GLM or generalized linear models. Right. I hope you are clear about the regression and classification algorithms now because we are going to use these concepts to develop the model and apply the model for newer datasets without writing a single line of code.

Accuracy in Classification and

In the previous chapter, we learnt about machine learning concepts. We also saw the different types of machine learning, classification and regression. In this chapter, we will see how to measure the accuracy of a classification algorithm and a regression algorithm. OK. What is accuracy? I am predicting someone will get a disease. Whether that person actually gets a disease or not is a measure of accuracy rate. So I compare what I predicted and what actually happened in actuality. That tells me about the level of accuracy. We are going to measure that as we're developing the model itself. So we get an idea of what is the kind of accuracy we can expect in our machine learning model based on historical data.

OK, so how will you measure accuracy in a regression problem? We use what is called an R square. Is R square the coefficient of determination? it is actually a ratio. We are going to see that very shortly. We also use one more metric. It is known as mean absolute error, while R square is a ratio of the difference between actual versus predicted, mean absolute error. tells the quantum of difference between actual vs predicted. So we will use both the coefficient and the absolute error to assess how good the model is. How good is the fitment? OK. That is a regression problem.

In a classification problem, We look at accuracy from the perspective of true positive and true negative, and we compare that with all the possibilities that can happen : true positive, true negative, false positive and false negative.

Right? Another metric that we use in a classification problem is what is known as the AUC area under the curve. This provides a range of values between zero and one. OK. It also uses all the four possibilities OK, and provides a value between zero and one. If AUC is closer to one, it means it is having a higher accuracy. if it is closer to zero means the accuracy is low, right? So now let's see. This R square and you see a bit more in detail.

OK? R-Square, as I mentioned, is a ratio. OK. It measures the residual sum of squares and the total sum of squares. So Y fitted, that you see here is actually the predicted value. OK. Residual sum of squares actually is the difference between actual vs predicted. Explained sum of squares is predicted versus the average. OK. So both I consider in the ratio using this formula. OK, I will have what is known as R square. If R square is closer to 100 percent or one, that means, you know, it's a great fitment, if it is 80 percent, the fitment is good. 40 percent, OK, I will say it is just below it and for the zero means there is no correlation. OK? Please note that R square can be negative. Also, that means. It is having a negative relationship instead of a positive relationship. You will have a negative relationship if R square is negative.

That is very much possible, right? Somebody studies for more hours. Unfortunately, that student scores less marks. That is, the more hours the student studies, the less number of marks the student gets. That is a case of negative correlation. Right. We don't want that, but we do have such scenarios in real life. OK. Now, let's see this. AUC, OK, area under the curve, we use what is known as confusion matrix, this is nothing but the matrix of predicted vs actual that is tabulation of true possible true negative, false positive and false negative. OK. We have already seen the explanation of false positive and false negative in the hypothesis chapter.

OK, so the confusion matrix is used to construct the area under the curve. OK. As I mentioned earlier, an AUC closer to one means high accuracy. Right? And the graph that you see here graphically shows how the area under the curve corresponds to a comparison between true positive and true negative. As you can see, the red is true negative green is true positive. If the area under the curve is closer to one, the overlap between true positive and true negative is lower. OK. As the area under the curve comes down, the overlap increases, which means the accuracy also comes down. Right. So are you understanding it? If you have a regression problem, you will use it. R square, if it is the classification problem, you will use the area under the curve right. And you will use these values, right, is it closer to one or closer to zero? And using that, you will determine how good the fit is, how good the accuracy is?

Developing and deploying churn prediction model in Vertex AI

In this chapter, we're going to see a classification model building. We are going to predict whether the customer will churn or not, that is whether the customer will lead the telecom services network or not. We are considering 18 independent variables, and the dependent variable is churn or no churn. It's a case of yes or no. That is why this is a classification problem. OK. The process that we are going to follow is the same as in regression. You've got the data set, we will determine whether it's a classification or regression model, in this case, it is a classification model. We will upload the data. We will choose the dependent or target variable, which is churn or no churn. Then we will run the model, then we will deploy the model. We will then use a dataset for predicting the future.

Let us first create the dataset. We have ensured that we have logged in into the vertex we click the dataset. That is the first step in any model building, so we give a name. We will be choosing tabular data because we are going to be discussing the classification model. OK, so let's name it, we will then come to tabular data, choose a regression slash classification and we will click Create. This will create the data set after this, we will have to upload the data. We will be uploading the churn dataset where both the dependent and independent variables are there. You have the option to upload the data from a cloud storage or from the query or from your computer.

I'm going to be uploading the data from my computer. Right. So let me select the file that is there in my computer, and I'm going to be uploading the customer churn data where details of both independent and dependent variables are there. OK. So I also indicate the path where this dataset will be stored in Google Cloud. OK. And post that I will click Continue for moving to the next step. I want to highlight that the cloud storage path is automatically chosen by Google Cloud. You can use the Browse option if you want to store this data in some other area of Google Cloud. OK. Data is getting uploaded once it is uploaded, it will take you to the next step. OK.

Once the data is uploaded, you can click generate statistics to see the extent of missing values that are there in the dataset and also the extent of distinct values. In this. The missing values are of particular importance because missing values will come in the way of developing the model. We should not have any missing values in our dataset. They must be replaced with either mean or median or mode, as the case may be. OK. So this process of generating statistics will take a little while. There is no missing data in our dataset, which is good. So we are good to go and start the process of training the modem.

OK. The first step in training the model is actually the training method, we reference the dataset that we're going to be using, then we're going to determine whether this is a classification or a regression problem. This is a classification problem. That is why we indicate the objective as classification. OK. We choose Auto ML and then click Continue. It'll take you to model details. where we indicate. Give a name to the model that we are building, and you choose the target column. The target column in this case. is about churn. That is the churn value. if it is a case of zero. It is churn. sorry if it is a case of one, it is, churn, if it is a case of zero, it is no churn, right? Then we click continue. But before that, let's see the options that are there.

We are going for a random assignment. That is the way in which data will be picked up for training. Validation and testing will be random, and this will be done automatically by Google Cloud's vertex environment. And we are choosing 80 percent for training, 10 percent for validation and 10 percent for testing. We are going for a random assignment. That is the split of training, validation and testing is done in a random manner by Google Cloud automatically. We are not going in for a chronological assignment. In fact, chronological assignment is not advisable.

Because chronological assignment will induce bias, bias will come in the way of accuracy of the model, nor are we going for Manuel because Manuel will be time consuming. OK, now we click continue here. We get to decide whether any of the independent variables should be removed or not. You see here, churn value is the. Target variable that is the dependent variable. we're going to predict churn, right. The rest of the variables are independent variables. OK, so you can decide whether any of the variables should be removed or not. You then click Continue. Here we decide the extent of duration for training the model. We'll go for the minimum. node hours. we will choose one and we enable early stopping also and click Start training.

OK. So please note that the process of training will take time. OK. And in fact, once the model has been trained, you will get an email to your registered email ID as to the completion of the process will be notified. OK. Please note again that this process takes time. Now, see that the model building has been completed, right? You see the green tick mark that indicates the model is ready for deployment. OK. We will now see the results of the model. We will get to see the level of accuracy we are getting in an area under the curve of 90 percent, which is good, right? Anything about 90 percent is always good. And as a value addition, we also get to see which of these factors are important. Right.

That is the big value addition in Google Cloud. You will see that shortly. OK? If you are having doubts as to what losses, what F1 score is. You can move your cursor over the question mark and you will see details about that metric. So this is the future importance that I was telling. This is a very useful feature in Google Cloud. If you have to explain the model to users, executives and other business people, it is always a challenging affair. This particular future importance graph will make the task a little easier. You can tell the users, executives and the business people that the most important factor is whether the customer has opted for internet service. tenure and must. So it makes the process of explaining the model to users a lot easier. Let me repeat again: there's a wonderful future.

Please use it. OK. So the model is ready now, we will go and deploy it. OK. The other point to note is, here we have chosen the confidence threshold of point five. OK. For the purpose of using the model on future data or other datasets, we first have to create a dataset. If you see, we created a dataset. At the beginning of this chapter and use the dataset to build a model, we have now built the model. The model is ready for deployment for the purpose of deployment. Also, we need a dataset, right? So that's what we're going to create. We're going to. Come to datasets, OK? Click Create Dataset choose Tabular Classification slash regression and then create the dataset. We will then upload the data. OK.

In this case, I'm going to upload the data from my computer. OK. That's what I'm doing here. Is this clear to you? And if you see here, I also renamed the dataset. OK. I created a data set at the beginning of the chapter for developing the model. The model is developed. Now I'm creating a dataset for deploying the model. So the model is deployed on this churn to the dataset. Right. Churn underscore to. So let me upload the data. And I also indicate where it will be stored. OK. I don't do any other activity. Right. The other point is to notice the column names in your dataset that you are using for deployment, right? It should be the same as the one that you used for building the model. If let's say you've used customer I.D.

as one of the variables. If customer id is stated as a single word. In the process of developing the model, you can't have customer underscore ID in. The dataset that we have used for deploying them on, please make sure. The normal feature should be the same. OK, this is an important point. Right. So the dataset that we are going to use for deploying the model is ready now let's come to a churn model that we developed earlier. We're going to. Deploy this model. OK. You have the option of. Either deploying this model as an endpoint for online predictions or we can use batch predictions that'll take a little longer.

OK. Batch predictions will take a little longer to get the results. Right. So we will click create batch prediction. We give it a name, then we choose the source, right? That we are uploading. We will also choose the location and the type of data. That we want as a result. We uploaded a CSV file. We are indicating the location of the CSV file. We want the output as the CSV file, and we're indicating the location where that output will be stored. That's what we're doing here. Right. We are indicating the location where the output file will be stored. In the file that is being used for deployment, I will have all the variables, all the independent variables, I will not have the dependent variable that is details of churn alone won't be there. The. Now, let me click Create.

And the process starts. As I indicated earlier, this will take a while. OK. You will get an email once the process has been completed. You see here. An email has come, indicating the process has been completed. I click the link and it takes you to the model area. OK. I click this and I will see the results. Remember, the results will be in the form of the CSV file, because that's what we opted for. OK, so you can see the location. So completed without errors that is indicated, if there are errors, it will say it has been completed, but with errors. OK. So we will get to see the results. We'll get to see the CSV file with an indication for propensity for churn whether the customer is likely to churn or not.

You will get to see the churn value. OK, see here the last two columns. Right. churn value is 0 score, churn value is one score. that is you get to see the results will be like point five, three something point four six something. If the value is closer to one, that means it is likely to have it. churn value, one means that churn is going to happen. churn Value zero means that churn is not going to happen. In the case that I'm highlighting now, the value for churn Value zero score is 0.7 one and the churn value one score is point two eight two something. That means the probability for no churn is 0.71 and the probability for churn is 0.28. Is this clear to you? churn value zero score is 0.71. The churn value is 0.28.

That means. The probability for churn not happening is higher. That means the customer is not likely to churn. Because the churn Value zero score is closer to one in this example. Let me explain this once again. In the example that I highlighted just now. We got a churn underscore zero value of 0.72, and churn underscore one value of 0.28. churn underscore zero corresponds to a scenario of churn not happening and churn underscore one corresponds to a scenario of churn happening. In this case, 0.72 is closer to one and 0.28 is not closer to one. That means churn will not happen. Yeah. Remember the word that I'm using? I'm saying the customer is likely to churn. I'm not saying the customer will churn. Probability can never be one. We are not talking in absolutes. We are talking in likelihood. Right.

What Next

You have come to the end of the program, I hope you like the coverage of the concepts and the case studies. I'll summarize the terminologies that we covered in this program, along with an explanation of the terminologies, and areas where you can apply. You can use this as a ready reckoner and this can clarify any doubt you may have on these terminologies. Finally, some movie recommendations for you. The Imitation Game is based on the real life story of Alan Turing. Alan Turing is considered as the father of AI.

This movie is about Alan Turing's role in breaking the Enigma code of Germany. As part of the Second World War. Person of Interest is an American drama series, wonderful web series on artificial intelligence. Catch Me If You Can is based on a real life story of a fraudster who goes on to work with the FBI and the banking institutions in the US to control and prevent fraud. Thank you. And best of luck.

7 Tweaks To Keep Your Website Looking Great!

The first thing I want to do is to establish in your mind the need for your own website. So I'm asking why you need your own website. Number one reason why you need your own website. It's about control. How many of us drive? We have a car yet we get on the bus. Why do we need a car if we can always get on the bus? Because sometimes you want to go straight to a destination you don't want to go on the bus because the bus has to stop at so many bus stops and you want to avoid that because you are under time constraints. The feeling of being in control when you drive your own car instead of getting on the bus is the same feeling you're going to have when you have your own website. You'll be in control of what happens in your business or to your business.

The second reason why you need your own website and this is probably even more important than control is that when you are on Facebook Instagram LinkedIn and any platform as your primary place of business when they make changes and they do update their Web site the Chengde algorithms that make so many changes at different times those changes can actually be detrimental to your business because those changes do not have you in mind. It has their own vision in mind or their own strategy in mind. And when those changes come you could find yourself being really out of pocket. So therefore the third reason why your own website is that you can maximize your cash. Nobody can tell you what to do on your own websites. Is this legal?

Of course nobody could tell you what to do so you can maximize your own products on your own website. And the fourth reason why you need your own website is because of creativity. If you want to start putting out your content with videos or you want to put out content that has links on it you want people to click to five lanes or ten links whatever it is you can do that you can use your own web site to learn how your marketing is really working or not working without your own site. You lose out on the ability to be creative and the ability to learn. And these are four major reasons why you need to have your website with an introduction. Opah persuaded you that even though you should keep your Facebook page and your YouTube channel you should be on Instagram or Pinterest or whatever else will come out after all that. But you must have your own website. I'll see you in the next chapter.

How To Construct A Winning Design Brief!

In this chapter we're going to talk about getting together a design brief and so we understand why it's so crucial to get a design brief. I want to illustrate this by sharing with you an experience I had a few years ago. Normally when we wanted to do designs we just screen got somebody and we said we want to do a fly or we want to put together a magazine and the person would say OK many pages is the magazine and we'll tell them what it is and we'll send them the text for the magazine and they'll put together a magazine and then we have to go through it and then add details and then change the colors and then you know really just go through a complete change from one sentence.

But then we began to use one company which was a well-known brand amongst the biggest companies even though they will work with small businesses but they generally work with big businesses. Do you know when we call them up and we say one wanted to design a flier? They said to us how long we want to have a meeting. For us to find out about your company, your business, your vision about where you're going in the future before we can even sit down to design a flier. And I thought that was a complete waste of time. But you know what. When they came to see us we sat down and they asked loads of questions and then went away and then began to work with us by first designing a flier for us. The flight wasn't exactly what we really really had in mind.

In fact the produced fly is better than what we could have ever requested. What's the difference between the two companies one works professionally you know that one does. Now when it comes to designing the website I want you to understand that most web designers are going to ask too much. Okay. And that's a problem as long as you know exactly what you want because you have to compose or put together what I want to look at. Now a design brief. OK. This will really help you. What's the first thing you want to look at when you're put into their design? You want to write down the purpose for your website. Why do you really want to set up a website?

I said my website because you want to become the industry leader or your market leader within your particular industry or you want to be the go to person within your niche. Why are you setting up your own website? You write a paragraph on that. The second thing you need to ask yourself is "What are the people that I want to reach?" What are the demographics? Are they between the ages of 20 to 25 or 20 to 30 or over 40s or over 50s or you know who are the people I'm trying to reach. And what are their Sadko graphics in terms of what their value was in the area of interest. What's their attitude to life? What are they open to receive?

You need to put that together also in a summary so that you understand who your web site is going to appeal to and that can come from the customers here that you're trying to attract. Then the third thing to think about very carefully is the types of products you are likely to sell on your website. Are you going to sell finished online Books are you're going to sell physical products because that will inform the theme you choose the lay out of your sites and pretty much where you host or how you host your content and the kind of plugins you are going to use and so many other things that is going to inform the shopping platform that you're going to use going forward. I think so.

Think carefully about the products that you're going to sell both now and in the future. And then the first thing to look at is to put together a list of all links of other websites that you really like because when you are talking to a designer you want to give them all this information. Were you given the purpose of your site or people you will now track the products that you are thinking of selling on your site? And Of course the content you're going to put on your site. Plus also you're going to look at you know these are the examples of the Web site that I like and I suggest you look at the market leaders look at what the market leaders are doing and then choose some of those Websites that you like and get your designer to have a look at those that's really important for them to come up with something that fits with where you are right now and also fits with what your ideal clients are looking for.

And then finally also really important aspects of the design brief is to take a long term view on how you're going to create your website. Do not let web designers rush you into creating a 20 page website. No, you're going to have a long term view. You might say well I'm going to create a four page website right now and then in a few months time I'm going to go for a second phase, phase two of it. Do not allow yourself to push down the alley of oh you've got to have all these bells and whistles right now. I think if you put together a design brief it not only helps you to carefully consider the way you are going as a web owner. It also helps your web designer to come up with a better website than they would ordinarily have created if you did not have a design brief that you presented to them.

And the third thing I think this is so important is because once you have a design brief it's easier for you to use contractors and easier for you to use people who are going to ask many questions we're not good at creating a website because you're going to direct them in the path you want them to follow. So that's what's going on. That's why it's crucial that you create a design brief before you start employing the expertise of a web designer. OK. All right I'll see you in the next chapter as we look at some colors that you might want to put into your design brief to season.

How To Choose The Right Colors For Your Website!

The colors you use for your website. Absolutely important because colors do communicate certain types of images in the minds of your clients and your customers. So choosing the best colors that represent your brand is absolutely essential if you think about websites that a lot of people just slapped close together without any major thought about what they're trying to communicate. Now I found an article online and I'm going to just read to you some other briefs on that particular article that helps you to understand the importance of colors in business. And I'm very glad I can tell you that if I go to my Website which is starting on business academy dot com.

You would see the kind of image they are trying to communicate and what the colors actually represent. So let's go through some of the colors and let's see what they represent. Red is a physical color which calls for action to be taken. Its high energy and strength draws attention to itself and demands to be noticed. Its high energy and strength draws attention to itself and demands to be noticed. That's why you would see that when it comes to pay now. Buy this now. The buttons and the pay boxes are generally red. That's why many oranges are in demand. Orange is a color of adventure which inspires and creates and Yasm it is optimistic and sociable and suggests affordability.

So if your website is related to you, you know if you want to communicate a sense of adventure and a sense of enthusiasm then you've got to use orange. What about yellow? Yellow is an illuminating and uplifting color which stimulates our analytical processes and assists with mental clarity. So if you take in things that are a little bit complex on your website where you want to use quite a bit of yellow so that you can communicate that ability to analyze to make what is complex very simple. Hey if it's green green is associated with natural health healing. It balances the emotions and inspires compassion. So depending on what your website is you need to choose colors that will truly represent and inspire your particular kinds. Talk wise balances and recharges the emotions and inspires good communication skills and self expression.

What about Blue Blue is the safety color to use in most applications. Implies honesty, trust and dependability. That's why your links are guessing what are in blue. Indigo is a powerful and strong color which conveys integrity and sincerity. It is associated with structure. It's got one or two more purple purple inspirations, wealth, quality fantasy and creativity. So your logo can actually carry the colors that represent what you're trying to communicate to your clients. Silver is a modern sophisticated color Kamin yet uplifting with a degree of mystery about it. What about Black. Black is the color of power and authority and in excess it can be intimidating and unfriendly.

What about white. White is a blank canvas waiting for creativity to be stimulated. It implies efficiency and simplicity, fairness and order. In a nutshell you've kind of seen how Carlos relates to the various aspects of our businesses and absolutely colors of a major. Colors are a major player when it comes to your website design. So really think about the colors you want to use for your logo for your pages for your content and let those colors be carried through in every aspect of your website. All right you go out of these colors. I really love it. See you soon.

How To Create A Perfect Calendar

In this chapter I want to look at your content calendar and this is another important part of creating a perfect website when you're thinking about your website. Initially you have to think about how much time you have to invest in your website because that will determine the amount of content that your website will hold or will have. Nothing is free really either. It costs you money. It's going to cost you time. So when you think about your Web site think about the content that you want your clients to actually read or to learn whenever they come to your site and I want to say that when you're thinking about content is more important to look at content from the from the perspective of the quality of the content rather than the quantity of the content. And in the long term quality always outshines quantity.

So if you want to put out a lot of plug content or text content on your website make sure even if it's frequent it's got to be quality. It's going to be very good quality stuff. Otherwise people are going to get turned off from coming to your site. So what I'm talking about is content though I'm referring to video content text content or links or whatever is suitable for your particular niche. E-books can be the content reports can be the content that you want to produce reports take longer time to create videos can take less time if it's just screen capture. But if it's recorded live videos you're going to go on camera like a talking head. It might take time to actually set up. So it may take time to create but whatever you are releasing on your site has got to be good quality. That's my main point right there.

The other thing to consider is the consistency out of turn. Are you going to release this content on your website? Some people suggest that you release one big content like a major report or a 50 20 10 page ebook or a content that is like 15 minutes or 10 minutes released or once a month or once every three months then have some other smaller content to go with it. It really just depends on what you have time to do. Even if you are using the services of a virtual person you still need the time to coordinate those kinds of activities. So you have to be consistent and determine where you're going to do what you're going to do every month, every two weeks, every week. Whatever it is or sometimes it will put our content every day because that's what that particular niche deserves or demands that you put our content every day.

So you might have to do that in practice. You are thinking about what your clients demand and the time that you actually have to release content on your website. And then finally to help you be consistent and help you to plan ahead you might just use a simple Excel sheet. There are lots of other paid calendars that you can buy. Call them content calendars but really when you are starting up a simple excel sheet that has the date the type of content and who is going to create content, what is the sufficient date the type of content and who is going to create it. Just those three columns can deliver you and help you to be more consistent than purchasing a card in the human eye. So start with a simple Excel sheet and if you feel that you want to do a little bit more than you can purchase a content calendar online. All right. I'll talk to you soon. Thank you.

Domain, Hosting and Platform - Choosing The Right One!

In this chapter I'm going to talk to you about domain name hosting and the platform. All right. All platforms nowadays are CIMS platforms which means content management system platforms and those types of platforms means that you can actually go up there and make the changes yourself. I'm going to look at that a little bit today as well. In simple terms domain is like the address of your house, hosting is like the land in which your house is built on and the house itself, the building and the utilities. I like the platform so if we think about the size of a car a car can be the domain of the car, the hosting is the chassis of the car and the structure of it and the engine and the interior is the platform that car uses.

The first thing I want to set is this. Do not use free hosting of free domains to build your website. When I say freedom I don't mean like maybe somebody like go daddies is giving you a free domain and then you're going to pay for the following year. So what I'm talking about. But what I mean is it's absolutely free. You're not paying for the domain name. You're never going to pay for a domain name. You're never going to pay for hosting those kinds of platforms can be very dangerous because if they go bust then you are left with nothing. So you want to be able to pay for your domain and pay for your hosting. What I mean is that it is so inexpensive today that you should absolutely consider paying for your domain and paying for your hosting because it doesn't cost that much. All right.

So let's look at some important features that I want to cover in this particular chapter. The other thing to say is that credibility is really important. Here are some examples of some good hosting Websites where you can purchase your domains. They are host to Go Daddy and Blue house. Now I think I learnt about blue hosts a while ago but the company that I've stayed with for the past 10 years that I've been on line has been host gator. I like those gators because I can call them up. The technical guys are really clued up. They're very friendly. There's no problem that I've called HOH's grateful that they've not resolved and they resolve it around the phone and if they have to go into a website or make some changes for you they'll do it.

So I'm a fan and I'm a fan of hosts gator these three hosting companies though are very credible. So blue host host gator and go daddy. So you can choose whichever one you want to go with. If you're going with an independent who is offering you to build a website and to host your website for you and help you to purchase your domain then make sure that those domains are in your name you have access to it and that they are also registered with one of the credible companies because an independent may have their own servers. So if they have their own servers and something happens to their servers then something happens. Your web site. You really want to consider this very well. Go with an established company.

That's what I would suggest. The other thing to think about when we talk about the platforms most of us have heard about is WordPress . I think it was one of the first kinds of platform that came out at what price is the CMOS that your web site uses. And there are other companies or there are other CMOS platforms that you can use like Drew. Paul Jumala, our media. We believe that most of the other ones. But here's the deal. If you are not familiar with Joomla or for example I suggest don't use it if you are not familiar with Wimbley just to use it. You know, I was reading an article right now that says like oh yeah. Joomla is like Wordpress. OK. It's like what. It's not what press I found WordPress to be the simplest type of platform you can use for your web. Meaning that if you can email you can text. Believe me you can use a WordPress site. It's that simple.

It's not really that easy to use because I'm not very technical but I build websites and I continue to update my site myself. Once you get going. You're going to want to make some changes yourself. You're going to want to put out an article if every time you want to make a change you've got to go to your web designer. It's going to cost you a fortune. You really don't want to do that. You want to use a platform that you are accustomed with. There are so many tutorials on how to use Wordpress or how to change your head and how to update that so much online. So my advice to you is use Wordpress. OK it could be a biased one but that's my advice. And then the final thing I would say is when you're starting your website you may have in your mind.

I really don't want to know how it works, I just want somebody to do it. I really want to know. Well that's not a good attitude for a start. Plus that's not true. I can tell you for sure. I used to be like that. And once you go away once you stop paying for design every time you want to change an image you start thinking for just a minute. Let me go up there and go make the change myself. So you've got to use a platform that you can make changes on yourself without needing to go to your web designer every single time. Well look I think there are going to be some complicated things that you are not able to do that you need to seek the expert help. Yes do so go back to your web designer when the issue is complex but for simple stuff learn to do it yourself because you can. So we've covered domains postings and platforms.

How To Outsource Effectively

You can outsource every part of the process of your website if you want to. It's from web design to content creation. You can outsource everything. You can even get somebody to find you the images to use and the thing that you want for your website can basically be outsourced. But outsourcing is also a tricky part of your web site perfection because if anything goes wrong then it affects the whole website or if you find yourself in the hands of somebody that can manipulate you or install something on your website that allows them to have a back door to your platform then you're in trouble. But that's only going to take place every once in a while. It's not something that I've experienced. I've heard stories about it but it's not things that I've actually been through.

It's all I can say I've been blessed with from being online. So let's look at some basic things about outsourcing. Number one is how do you find a designer. How do you find a designer? The best way that I can advise you to find a web designer is by getting a referral. Somebody who has used that particular web design before. Before you go on the platforms before you go to look at Websites I'm going to tell you about in a moment. Try and find a friend, an acquaintance or somebody who can refer you to a web designer that they've used. Somebody has created a site you know off that's the best way. And I think you should try to locate your web designer.

The second thing is when it comes to web design or content creation here are some sites that you can use up to work Eldon's five look at their logos right there. They are the companies that I've used. I think I've used elands or new ones. Yeah I've used Elance ones. I've used up work recently but I've used five or lots and I'm going to show you the strategy when you're going to use any of these Websites what to do and how to do it. There are lots of good platforms out there but I'm just talking about the ones that I've used and I know that they work. So what's the strategy for actually using these external sites for your web design or your content creation.

The first thing I would say is always start small. If I wanted to do a 20 page website and I'm just trying out a designer I'm not going to design a 20 page website straight away. I'm going to chop it down to bite size and say why don't you just create the front page or the home page and let me have a look at that. And then you know we go on to the next four pages so that space and the work out that I may be in control of what the web design is doing. If I want to write the book for example and I'm going to outsource that eBook creation I'm going to start by telling the content creator to write two pages first let me have a look at it because I want the option of being able to access it if it's not going quite as well as I want to. So the first thing to do is to start small.

The second thing is to test that kind of work and then hand test them by getting them to do something small like I said earlier. If it's a case of you want them to work to a particular deadline they need to test that out with the person before you commit larger work to them. Test the platform to make sure they understand you and they fit in with what you're trying to do. Make sure they want to work with you. I think on the experience ones with one of the platinum I'm going to mention the name because that's just one experience. The guy I asked him to design my website at first I just didn't have a clue about what he was doing. Every time he worked on the website it brought me more issues to have to deal with. And in the end I just kind of counsel that you know because I just couldn't work with him.

And I learned then that the problem was I committed a large amount of work into his hands that I would never do that again. So if I'm using something for the first time I'm definitely going to test them. Plus the first try I found that works with me. For example if you go on to 5. There are people who can deliver in one day. People will deliver in three days, it will deliver in 10 days, we will deliver in 15 days. I'm not going to work with you if you deliver in 15 days or seven days. No, because I've done that before. And what happens is when you come to work somebody may write a piece or conjure up 500 word content.

Somebody should be able to get back to you in three days when you allow the content creator to deliver a work in seven days and then on the seventh day they can, so that's wasted one whole week. So you do want to do that. You want to find somebody who can deliver in two days one day a maximum of three days especially if you're working with them for the first time. For a simple amount of work. OK. If you're writing an ebook that takes a 30 page eBook like one to use for your content then you really want them to take their time to write this so being able to write over a week or two that's quite good. Apart from getting you to change my home page and insert a head on it or something. I have to tell them it's going to take seven days because that's the way that you work. I don't want to work with you. I want people to

deliver quickly because if they can so on you because something happens in their lives that they need to just cancel the work or something unfortunate happens that you want to be able to have the option of hiring someone else to do the work. So those three things are really important. Start small tests and use shorter periods of delivery. Ok so today we kind of looked a little bit about outsourcing. You can go on these Websites or work. Come on, come on 5. Come on, you will find good. There are some excellent people on fiber and there are some who just don't know what they're doing. You have to test a variety to come up with the best one for you. And when you find it. Finally I'm going to say this when you find somebody who is really good. I suggest you treat them well, give them tips and make sure they stay with you for a long time. All I see said.

What Are The Right Tools To Use

In this chapter we're going to look at a variety of tools you should use for your website and I'm going to do this in maybe three categories. The first category are tools to do with images and design. The second is to do with getting the right keywords that you can use for your content. And the third area is really endeavoring to post content that is already very popular online so posting content is already popular on social media. So let's look at the tools now. I've kind of picked this down to the essentials. So it's not so much that I need to know about six different tools I need to use but I'm just saying use this once.

So the first two tools I want to look at are COME BACK TO COME AND GET stem so Stansel come will cost you nine dollars a month to use this platform and they can pretty much do what converter—does with nine dollars a month. You have access to lots of wonderful beautiful images and you can create your own images or you can get the images you need to send to your web designer for your web design thinking about the colors that you want. This is really about you taking control of your website. OK. You send your designer the images you want or give them access to a book of images that you have that you know fits with your website or when you want to write a content you can send your designer the image that you want to put in that content so you have control of your content.

Like I said, it is nine dollars a month and you will have access to all of that. But my favorite one I use very well is convert or come since I was referred to so one of my friends called Dunkley naturally introduced me to convert. I didn't know it existed since he told me this two years ago about a year and a half ago. Now I've been using canvas. And I love Canada. You can develop your Facebook headers on it. You can do your Twitter head as you can do your website headers any kind of social media header and email. You can create it on convert or come. And it's so easy to use. Then I'll give you different options in which you can download your images.

So whether it's going to be a PDA as a P N G or jpeg images are superb. They always look good on your website convertor. Come will cost you $1 per image and you can put text on the image. But every image you use is one dollar. I think the downside of using Cambre for me is that once you download the image you're only allowed to make changes to the image within 24 hours. Otherwise after that you'll have to pay. You have to pay another one dollar to get the set image. So the best thing to do is first Arite pays $1 dollar. They may enter into a folder then you go back and then you can put a text that you want on the image because the converter also has an option whereby you can upload an image and put text on the image without it costing you any money.

So once you buy the image you download on your computer then you go back onto Kanva and change the make you still going to pay the same one dollar or just one one time one dollar per age but then later on if you want to use the same image for something else which is very likely you can then go up and upload the image when the options are there to cover the come is the one when it comes to images for your content and images for your site. The second group of tools I want to talk about is or are tools to get the right keywords. Keywords are still very important for your discovery online for people to find the content for Google to index you so that you can appeal or get traffic that you want you can generate organic traffic. You still need to create content based on those searches that people are making.

So LSI grafter come keyword to dot I go on the Google Keyword plana are the ones I've used to generate keywords so all these tools are free. By the way apart from cover and get stenciled come cover the cost is one dollar per image and the LSI graph dotcom and key word to. I go and google keyword planner they're all free to use before Google kills planning to be registered on the platform for you to be able to use the key that Pana used to be free for you to just use it. But now they get it and they get smart so they get you to register to actually use the Q or planner. They might even get you to pull your credit card details in your card details. Before you can use the keyword plan.

But they will not charge your card. So it's a very good tool to use obviously because it's Google. Then Google knows what people are searching for so they can generate keywords and then write articles or content or create videos or create infographics based on the keywords that you have discovered. OK. Like I said Key words could be such phrases or words that people that really know you want to relate to are searching for online. So what these tools do for you is to give you a group of keywords that you can actually write content with yourself or create content. So it's really really good. And then finally getting to share content that is already popular right now.

But sumo was referred to me or I discovered BAA's sumo does come from Nil's Patel so you need to check out Neil Patel. Neil Patel is one of the people I follow online. Marketing online is superb when it comes to content and you get a lot of value from just reading that stuff. Anyway he talked about both Zumo and till now I've just sent a message to my designer to actually post for me a content that I discovered on Barsoum So let me tell you I was if you go to buzz Zoom Zoom—. It will allow you to search for any phrase and then it will give you the top 10 free top 10 most used content that relates to that phrase. So if I search today for example business plan templates and they give me like 7 different content that is being shared online, the first one was written by a guy at Inc to come and that's been shared over two thousand nine hundred times so I'm basically going to re-post the content on my website.

Obviously declaring the source and giving and giving credit to those who have discovered the content from you know full disclosure stuff. But the point is you are reaching a new audience with that same content that is already popular and because it's already a popular one you can share it all too. You can write something similar to it. Sometimes I may go to Bob Zumo and discover that there's a content that says oh 10 ways to create a perfect business plan. So I said OK that's cool. I want an hour right. 15 ways to create a perfect business plan because the idea is you can just recreate it and create better content than what is already existing. And by doing that you are more likely to run.

As time goes on in the organic searches for the same keyword So Buzz them all is free. So Geller I don't know how long it's going to be free for but it's free for now. So use it. And then finally I want to say this always starts small. Don't try to, you know, maybe buy 100 images because you don't know what images you're going to need really. So do it slowly have a long term view on what you do and take control of your website get content from Canada home or get stenciled or come get keywords from LSI graft or come Oakie what to dot com Google killer plana and then content that's already been shared online that is popular get it from both Zumo dot com. All right.

How To Effectively Promote Your Content

Welcome back to this chapter. I want to talk to you about promoting your content, what you need to do, why you need to do it and who you need to do it with. OK. Let's get started. Number one reason why you actually need to promote your content is that you want to quickly and effectively get in front of as many people as possible and you want to get your website generate in traffic as quick as possible and as much as you possibly can because that's the only reason because you want to reach more people you want to reach a particular type of audience and you want to make sure that your content is in their face because there's so much content out there that if you're not effectively promoting what you're doing then you're not going to get in front of the audience that you really want.

So you need to make sure and organically without any kind of activity behind it it's going to take so long to happen. So you want to promote what you're doing. Where do you promote this? Well the best place to start is by using the emails of people that you already have to let them know that hey I've put out a piece of content here and this is what it can do for you and this is how you can benefit from it. So go to my Website and read it. Once you've created a Web site or when you are in the process of creating that Website you actually need to install an email management system like something like a web or MailChimp are two popular ones that use a webcam and MailChimp dot com. They're quite popular and they're quite good.

They're good for different things. But my favorite one is a Web site. That's what you use to generate your sign up forms so that people can sign up to your content or to receive a piece of content from you or better piece of content. Let's say one thing that I do is I'll put out content and I'll then have a download sign up button that says if you want the PDA version you can collect it by giving me your email. And sometimes people respond to that and that way you keep generating emails of people who are interested in the type of content that you're putting out. So therefore when you create any content you can inform them that hey guys there's a new content on if you're a member of a social media like Facebook or Instagram then that people now that you've just released a piece of content you can get your friends to send out an email for you if they have a group of people there that they have influence with to also come over and read your content.

And finally one of the things I've done in the past is I would promote my content with advertising so I might create a YouTube video and now promote it with a YouTube video ad. OK. So that would generate a lot of traffic to my YouTube page and also to my website. Those are some of the ways where you can promote your content. Another thing that I've done is I'll use five dot com to find somebody who does press releases and I'll get them to send the press release of my content to a variety of sources. Maybe they'll send it to 250 press release companies or 250 Web site Daswani We have also promoted. OK. But you know you've got to promote what you're doing.

And how do you do this? Well like I said eazy e-mails and using a company like five or like I said and nothing that I do is you can send out text and you can use your Worksop. Let's not forget that you can create webinars around the subject so that people can sign up to the web and listen to a little bit more of what you have to say and then go over and download that content from your Website. So that could be one of the ways to do it because I've done that also before and definitely one of the ways that I get my content I like S.E. earlier is to create a PDA. One of the reasons why I create a PDA is that in the PDA I can insert cells like. All right. So that's another good thing.

Why you create a PDA document is because you can insert cell links in there so that somebody who's done a PDA can actually go over and buy some of your products as well. And then the final thing is with hope. Well what I've done because I'm going to meet up with a group . I've started working with some of the other meetup hosts to create events. Right. And from creating events I want to get us to do content together. Or if I read a piece of content by somebody I might say to them well can we work on this together. For example on my UDMA page there's a lady that I've been creating Book content with called Lara Fabians.

Now I just meld shots. Lara Fabians and we got talking and we kind of thought oh you know what I said to you know can we create Books together and we've done about four or so Books together right now. And the reason the relationship is working quite well is because we create Books together that we put on our Web sites and we can pray on our own on you and we're selling the Books and that's how you can create content also for your website. I mean I'm going to use that content and use the content I'm going to use on my website. So working with people of like minds is really good because they are promoting you and you're promoting them.

So I'm talking about Lara Fabian's now and she also talks about me when she when she does her own stuff with some of her own clients so you're going to be working with people that can extend your brand beyond what you can do creating content with other professionals within the field is an absolute for you to get your name and your content out there. All right then. See you soon.

Homeopathy Overview

The reason that I teach this particular class Introduction to Homeopathy is because despite the success and the safety of homeopathy as a respected form of medicine in the world here in the United States we're still asking or meeting people every day that say what is Homeopathy and how come I've never heard of it and if it really works is it safe? And what is it about homeopathy that differentiates it from herbal supplements and seeing a naturopath or an acupuncturist? Or for that matter, what's the difference between getting conventional medical treatment? So the reason I'm here tonight is to be able to introduce you to homeopathic principles. The best way to learn about homeopathy really from the beginning is to learn a little bit about medical history. So I'd like to expose you to a little bit of that tonight.

But I'd like to know why you're here. Is there anybody in the room tonight? That's familiar with homeopathy, that has used homeopathy? Is this a new word for you, a new concept? Does anybody have any questions or can you tell me what brought you here tonight. My brother has ALS "I want to learn more about natural treatments" Great. Thanks for coming. Go ahead. Yes hello. Yes. OK. Any familiarity with doing what's considered non-conventional or alternative medicine? I'm feeling like we kind of need to take this on ourselves. OK. All right thanks for coming. Anybody else with a question or comment? You're grinning. You got something? Somebody's arm twisted? OK.

Did you have a question? I heard about your vaccine kit. I haven't vaccinated my children yet. OK. I suddenly become allergic to things. I've broken out in eczema. I wondered if there were any natural remedies to heal that? OK. OK. Thanks for coming tonight. Anybody else with a question you want to make sure we cover? Yes. Is it auravedic? Indian Medicine. Yes. Does that have any similar theories? All alternative medicine has a similar theory. So if we take medicine as a group and we look at medicine as a big pie we get divided. Conventional medicine with alternative medicine and the difference truly is our intentions and our tools.

So if we were to travel along this line, being in health inside the circle, healthy happy content sleep could meet our goals. When we get stressed let's say that we get a letter big bill in the mail that makes us worried and we don't sleep then it's worry, don't sleep cranky irritated and then it becomes something like the extension of this being an ulcer and on an antidepressant or antianxiety drugs and miserable or unhappy or developing things like allergies. The more we medicate when we do traditional medicine the further we get away from balance so we get some relief in the moment. But there are side effects to these drugs and we increase our disease over time.

If we do alternative medicine when we get out of balance or begin to manifest pathology mentally and physically. What happens is that acupuncture, Ayurvedic medicine, naturopathy, homeopaths, what we're looking to do is move you back toward a state of balance. So we want to minimize the symptoms and we want to medicate you less and less. We want to move the state of totality back to a place where you're healthy and happy. So in the case of Medicine what we're doing is we're treating her Medicaid and giving relief in the moment. Some of these drags last like pain relievers for hours if you're lucky and you have to repeat the dose. You don't necessarily it doesn't heal back pain.

It just makes you not feel the pain OK. That's that. That's medicating when I'm going to use something like a homeopathic remedy like Arnica. That works as an anti-inflammatory. It gives us relief that's permanent. So the next day we'll be in less pain. And the next time we repeat it we're in less pain. So we need not only less but to solve the problem we don't ongoingly medicate. So in alternative medicine every field in what we call alternative medicine is working toward a common goal. We work well together with chiropractic massage therapy. All of us are looking to move you to a better state. OK. When we medicate let's say that we're doing high blood pressure medicine.

What we have to do is every 12 to 24 hours you have to take that drug and the effect of the drug is what we call suppression which is the enemy of us in the group of us to do all alternative medicine if we don't want to create a suppression we don't want to cover it up. We'd like to resolve it. So the side effects of taking a high blood pressure pill every day over a 10 or 20 year period could be things like congestive failure and an enlarged heart. So what we want to do is not go that direction. Now with the AMA does in my opinion that's genius and where their talent truly lies and the use of their education is an emergency medicine. If any one of us got run over by a truck that's where we're headed. OK. We're going to be sewn back up. We want that emergency care.

And it's that nothing offered like it with their tools and their facilities. What physicians also are able to do in this country is surgery whereas most of us who do alternative medicine can't own a scalpel much less use it. So they do surgery. The other thing that they have that we don't have is their diagnostic tools. So they have MRIs and blood tests. They have ultrasounds. Some really great tools. The tools are used diagnostically and things like oriental medicine, we can use some of the maps on our bodies, we can use feet like a reflexologist would do our tongue diagnosis like the Oriental medicines do, we can use iridology for the people who are into doing that level of diagnostics.

So they have lots of diagnostic tools but not on the same level as the machines that are provided or the doing things like a CT scan. So what the AMA does poorly is treatment once you get diagnosed with things like diabetes or infertility or high blood pressure the only tool they have is medicating So it doesn't resolve the problem it just gives you momentary comfort or momentary and could be in the case of you know high blood sugar and high blood pressure that may be lifesaving in the moment but over time it's detrimental to your health. So what we shine at is resolving problems minimizing treatment or actually like I said altering your state so that your blood pressure comes down.

Whether that be from diet or nutrition or a homeopathic remedy we're looking to move the opposite direction. And that's what really splits us. Does that answer your question? Yes. And brought another question. Sure. So arnica, you're using it, so you're using something. Yes. You say it'd take care of your back pain not just for today. but for.... You can resolve the , you can also resolve the fact that you don't hold a chiropractic adjustment homeopathically. We can deal with chronic disease as well as acute diseases. So, the medications...because both of them are medications... That's not true. All right. So in the realm of homeopathy we don't want to, and I can teach you and show you the differences. About the difference in medicating and resolving a problem.

So I like to use this tree diagram that I drew when I was in school 20 years back. When we look at this tree the tree has a root and that root really is about what we know of medicine is genetic predisposition. The root is going to determine whether you're blond hair blue eyed or whether or not you're a large boned or have a predisposition to heart disease so this genetic predisposition exists for the tree as well. It's going to be a rosebush or an oak tree. Above that we have the influences on health which are diet and environment and in this particular case for the tree it's whether the trees are overcrowded, whether the soil is any good, whether they get enough water or whether it's a parasitic environment or not.

These things have an influence on health. Diet and environment are really the only tools that we have any control over. It's not uncommon for a physician to say or recommend that you move to Arizona if you have asthma that you'd be less irritated in that environment. It doesn't get rid of the asthma, it just aggravates it less. You can also see that in this part of the country as well. How about you move out of the moldy basement. It's aggravating your breathing or creating bronchitis or issues with pneumonia and allergies. So we can adjust to this environment. We can put HEPA filters on the house so I don't know how that saves you when you go outside in the spring but it has an influence on our health.

It may minimize the aggravation in the case of diet. We can eat good food, we can eat bad food, you can drink like a fish, you can smoke. Those things influence us in a positive or negative way. The problem with trading at an influential level is that it's a lot of work. So what happens is that if you've been advised not to drink milk, don't eat chocolate, don't eat sugar white flour, stay away from gluten. What happens is either you're not happy anymore or the minute you cheat the result is that now the disease is your fault that you have indigestion or that you have allergies or that you have gas and bloating. OK.

So this gives us some level of control of these influences on health. From this place, this genetic predisposition, who we are, we come through those influences and then we can poke out symptoms when we do that if we treat and medicate them they mutate to a new form. So medicate means to cover up using something synthetic in our environment in the United States means it's been patented and owned by a company that profits by the fact that you're going to take that pill. They are giving you relief of the symptoms knowing that ultimately it has a consequence. All right so here's what happens is if we take a healthy child as an example we're going to vaccinate them when we put the disease matter in their body the body starts to react and they get a fever.

So they get cranky weepy, feel lousy and get that fever. The body's trying to fight that contagious material off. So when that happens and we use some Tylenol it shifts it. Now to hear the child now gets a rash so he's red hot irritated. Now on the skin instead of having a fever say if we take and we rub some cortisone cream on there what happens is the next time the child gets sick it's something worse like asthma. So now we're going to put that inflammation down in the lungs and what are we going to use to treat asthma. Get some more steroids that'll work. So we're going to use some steroids and we're going to treat and medicate every time the child can't breathe while they are continuing to have less and less good health. OK. We've now created a chronic disease instead of an acute problem.

So now what happens is that after we've used the steroids for a breathing problem then what happens is they develop a more serious skin disease like eczema. So now you're going to see chronic skin disease and what are we going to put on that some more steroids? So what they do now is play cat and mouse. They alternate until they're into young adulthood by using their inhaler or treating that skin condition. So now what happens is that supposedly after all these years of suppressing covering it up medicating medicating medicating. Now when they get into adulthood, instead of growing out of it which is what we're told happens now we're going to have chronic sinus problems and allergies the rest of our life.

So we've just moved the disease around making it deeper and deeper and more and more chronic. So the depiction of that is that we have these two scales representing our vitality. We have our scale from zero to 100. This side is the vitality of the said disease and we split our life force between them. So what happens is that if you're not feeling good, overstressed , don't go to sleep, drink too much wine the next morning and you're going to feel lousy. So we're going to have pathology on the side we're down to 90 /10. Now if you get some sleep take some vitamin C sip on your echinacea, whatever it is you're going to do, go to bed early. The next night you probably will recover.

If you medicate it you maintain it. So the more that we medicate or do things like inject vaccine disease material into the body to be able to fight that off in our immune system to be active in defending it. We lose vitality and it lowers our vitality. Now what happens is that the evidence of this is that the kids are unhappy they're snotty belligerent. They're hard to get along with when people don't feel good. The evidence that this theory is true is that any one of these things that we can undo and remove comes back so that we can actually use homeopathy to eradicate disease. We're not just medicating the state of it. We actually can undo it.

So if we go back to our drawing here and we actually go back and annotate the ill effects of vaccines then this resolves. So if we get disease where its origin is we actually can shift the state of vitality. So it's different from medicating. If you want to use homeopathy and herbs and supplements and acupuncture we can treat all these things acutely. We can go to the use of a remedy for pain relief. You can go to acupuncture when your heels hurt and you can't stand on them in the morning. You can take coenzyme Q10 and some fish oil because you're afraid you're going to have a heart attack. We can make some red rice yeast. We can start medicating all of our body parts.

We can do that with homeopathy. We can do it with herbal medicine, we can do it with any form of treatment where every time something's wrong you go running and try to fix it. The difference is that we're not creating a suppression. We're taking care of it at the moment and we're getting relief for the moment. The potential and the glory of homeopathy for all of us who practice classical homeopathy is to look at this totality of symptoms go what the heck is wrong here. What can we do? Can we go in and clean up this never well sense so that we can give this person relief instead of treating allergies so that you're not taking a homeopathic remedy every time you're snotty, or having to take herbs every day to build up your immune system. How do we just go in here and clean this mess up?

So we look at it a little bit differently. The potential of homeopathy is a little bit unique. We see classical work done in acupuncture to some degree if they are trained classically but they have that potential. They're taking account of what your organs are doing and what your manifestations are, not just the symptom. So if we go in here and we say let's annotate the ill effects of the vaccine and wipe this out so we don't have to medicate it. Then we're looking at this, gee, you have some issues with circulation or getting a little bit breathless not the vitality you used to have.

We can say gee if there's a genetic predisposition toward heart disease how about if we direct our remedy to that genetic predisposition. We can look at somebody in their totality mentally and physically. So the minute you're not afraid that's your first clue you're in better health. The second one is to get rid of the blood pressure or the high cholesterol or whatever it is that you might be doing that shows that you have disease and actually get rid of the symptoms because we're healing it not because we're medicating it.

Part 2: Introduction to Homeopathy

So the glory of all of us who have done any kind of classical homeopathy as a patient and gotten results is that it's for the most part considered permanent. And I'll give you an example. I was a fairly unmedicated child. I wasn't sick very often. And when I got into adulthood and active as a businesswoman I was busy enough not to notice that I hit 30 without ever getting pregnant. In the meantime I'd made my normal visits to the gynecologist. And despite the frustration level of not getting any good answers about what was a malfunction junction for me, or pains or different problems that I had through the years, my body obviously wasn't working right and I wasn't making any progress.

So after using the conventional tools to tell me things with an ultrasound like you have cystic ovaries or maybe your blood shows your hormones aren't completely perfect. The offer to me was to do surgery or to be given chemicals and that wasn't appealing to me. I said you know there's a belief that I have that I should be able to get my body healthy or I should be able to function normally. So I got a referral from one of my subcontractors who said that they had tried an infertility doctor. So I went to see this infertility doctor and the first question she asked me is how much meat do you eat. And I said eat a lot of chicken. She said you'll never ovulate; it's full estrogen.

So she wanted to load me up on chemicals too but I bailed out of there and went straight to the health food store which I frequented and I asked the woman for a book or a referral about nutrition. So I began to read about nutrition. I changed my diet. I did everything that you could possibly do that was probably off the deep end. I went to a macrobiotic camp for a week and learned how to eat rice and seaweed. You know you name it I tried it and the result is that I did get healthier but I didn't get pregnant either. So ultimately my husband came down with the shingles. And by now I've done the kahuna healer, the acupuncturist the naturopath you name it I tried it.

So she said when did you see a homeopath and I thought you know here in my opinion it was just one more nut. And an investment. It's not cheap either. So I went to take my husband to this big commercial clinic in downtown Los Angeles. It was quite a ride for me. And he went and he sat on the table there on the exam in the exam room with his shirt off and the doctor walked in and took a look and went man you have shingles. You're going to have it every time you're stressed out. The pain can last for months or years to come And here, have some cortisone cream. I said wait a minute. I had a little card in my hand. I said I'm here to see this homeopath. He said Oh he said I'm in the wrong room.

He left, and the homeopath came in. He takes one look at him and he goes man that's pretty painful but don't worry it'll be gone in a couple of days and won't come back. I said whoa! So he wrote us a prescription. We went down to the homeopathic pharmacy and filled it and he did really well with it. So I called this doctor back on the phone myself, the homeopath and I said I'd like to make an appointment. So then I went in to see him and they sat me in his office. Which I thought was peculiar. So he asked me what I was doing there and I began to boo hoo and told him I was there for infertility and he said began to ask me questions and I would say that that went on infinitely, a couple of hours he asked me what I consider to be were multiple unrelated to my situation moron questions and at the end of that he wrote me a prescription for a remedy. So I went down. I bought a homeopathic remedy. I told the pharmacist I'm not putting that in my mouth.

The guy is whacked and I want to know exactly what it is. Before I touched it he never looked between my legs. Didn't do an exam that seemed far out to me. So I took my book and I opened it. Luckily for me he sold me a good book and I was able to assess and look up the remedy and see what it was and what it did. And in our materia they list what the remedies are made from and what the mental and physical symptoms are by body parts so it lists the problems , all the negative problems that you might have mentally and then good goes down your head , ears , eyes , nose all the way through all your bodily functions.

And I had most of them which really irked me because I couldn't figure out how he could assess that from the dumb questions he asked me. But I thought about the hay. I tried it and I felt like a million bucks. So the interesting part about that is I go back to work and I'm a busy woman. I had 25 employees and was busy, k. So I got pregnant pretty fabulous and I didn't really attribute it to homeopathy until I got pregnant immediately after. So then I realized that my body not only worked but what was fixed was you know obviously no longer broken. So I have two girls they're now 21 and 22. They've never been to a medical doctor their entire life. That's not true. I had them in a home birth and I did have an old physician that backed up that home birth and did some more baby checkups with him.

But the kids haven't seen a doctor since. They've never had a cavity. They've never had an antibiotic, they've never had a dose of Benadryl. So homeopathy is not a casual thing to me. I have a passion for it. I wanted to raise my kids healthy. I wanted them to have great diets and the best food I could afford. So I moved to Montana. The girls had some good open spaces and we were able to raise some of our own meat. And I'm really lucky. So it works for me. When I moved to Montana I didn't know a soul. And I started working on the neighbors and anybody that I could offer help to including their animals. And I've been teaching homeopathy ever since. So this is my 18th year in private practice, my 16th year of teaching and I teach every level of homeopathy wherever the questions are, whatever the style of the group is, whether it be practitioners or whether it be a group of chiropractors or massage therapists or moms.

Homeopathy is useful in each and every one of those levels. So what I'd like to do is tell you a little bit about what Homeopathy really is and what makes it different and what sets it apart from things like herbs and diet type therapies that you might be familiar with. Homeopathy started about two hundred and twenty years ago in Europe by a physician by the name of Samuel Hahnemann and Samuel Hahnemann was a chemist and an educated man who was multilingual. And his frustration with the kind of medicine that they were doing in his day motivated him to ask more questions. He was a deep thinker in my opinion and a philosopher as well and said things like why is the use of medicine or treatment making people less healthy in the long run.

Why is their long term quality of life not as good as it was before we medicated them? So the medications of the day included things like silver nitrate and for any of you who use colloidal silver it still falls in that category for using mercury we still use that in our teeth as well as a defoliant and things like our irrigation systems even knowing it's a known poison they did breadletting and breadletting was not at all unpopular we actually lost George Washington here in the United States by bloodletting for tonsillitis. So these treatments of the day turpentine for things like bronchitis or pneumonia things like tar for eczema. I mean they were really pretty barbaric.

Now Hahnemann said that this wasn't really making him very happy or very comfortable and he actually quit practicing medicine. He went back and hit the books and began to translate the scientific and medical journals. And for a living to feed his family he began to write about disease and philosophize where disease was coming from at that particular time the beliefs of the day included things like that disease was actually a curse or some kind of punishment. So they didn't understand about genetic predisposition. They did not have microscopes to look at bacteria in pond water. They had no idea the difference between a bacteria and a virus like we have the privilege to do today.

Say he wrote about things that he perceived to be a problem and that there was in fact genetic predisposition. I drew that for you in the tree that there was some reason that people were more vulnerable or susceptible to disease. We still use all of his philosophies today by the way in the medical manuals we still make reference to those names. He gave genetic predispositions in the categories of the diseases that they are. And he also said that there's a contagion and there's some reason that people get sick. He brought inroads to medicine. We still use simple things like washing your hands. If there were germs or bacteria and you went from woman to woman like a gynecologist or an obstetrician would today that more women died by birth's medical deliveries than they did by midwife deliveries because they were contaminating one woman to the next by not doing things as simple as washing their hands.

So when Hahnemann was able to teach the doctors and scholars of his day things that he was able to observe, medicine began to change and evolve. Now what Hahnemann did too as well, he was reading other people's works. There were concepts that recurred like, like could cure like, or using minimum doses were as are not more medicinal than the strong powerful doses of drugs or poisons that they were using as medicine. So Hahnemann got his opportunity to give that a try during a malaria epidemic and malaria is commonly treated by quinine and on that day it was known as cinchona bark, but the extract out of cinchona bark is quinine as we use it today. But Hahnemann took that quinine and he got sick as if he had malaria.

So he repeated the experiment when it wore off and he got the malarial symptoms again so he treated his colleagues as well as his family and guinea pigged them and they all got sick as if they had malaria. So he was spurred on at that particular point to try other substances but the deduction was that what we're using to treat could also cause disease symptoms. So what happened is that he also discovered that in this theory being able to try the poisons of the day which were medicines we don't want to take I or my children if I was experimenting to try mercury. We already knew it was poison, he didn't want to eat that along with turpentine and anything else if they were using as poison the poisonings of plants of Bella Donna or arsenic.

Not a popular idea to want to take that home to your wife or your family. So what Hahnemann did is he diluted the remedies down or the substances down and produced from a physical substance and now we today call a remedy and how he accomplished that was by taking the original substance in the lab and remember that Hahnemann was a chemist. so this is completely natural to him but we're going to use the substance arsenic and what Hahnemann did was diluted the substance or made it or actually made it soluble he dissolved it and made it soluble. We refer to that as the mother tincture of pharmaceutical zero.

If we weren't using arsenic and we were going to use something like chamomile or any other squeezing of a plant or could even dissolve and mix soluble metals or minerals we refer to that as mother tincture. Now to make a remedy what happened was that Hahnemann took these sterile vials put a hundred drops of water in each and every one of them and began the dilution process he removed one drop of arsenic and put it in that first hundred drops of water and then shook it hard with a lid - the process we call succussion is shaking vigorously or pounded. Now when you remove that finish preparing that first dilution we remove one drop into the second.

So in math we're going to refer to that as one of a hundred to the second power. We're going to take out time the second to the third and shake it from the third into the fourth, five to six, when we get to six we refer to that homeopathically as the potencies 6C. What that means is that we end up with one over a hundred to the sixth power. OK. Now that dilution if I do it at half strength or half dilution is that we end up with one over a hundred to the sixth power is one followed by 12 zeros if we use six zeros we get one part per million. So it's much more diluted if I put the other six on there. But for our sake we're going to call this diluted at least one part per million. It does not mean 6CC like it would if you were going to fill a syringe or measure volume.

In homeopathy the potency is how many times the substance has been diluted. Now the next thing that Hahnemann did that was really unique once he got these materials into a safe potency is that he now tried them on humans. We're going to give this arsenic now to a control group as we do today. And I said Hahnemann guinea pigged his colleagues and his family to do this. But what happened was that when he gave them arsenic without telling them what it was ask them to document how they felt. What they said was I feel like I've been poisoned. I want to know what you gave me. I don't trust you for a minute. I don't feel good. I don't like this. It's making me feel like I have burning in my throat or when you know in my—when I go to the bathroom I'm not happy with this. I think that you should stay right here with me and you know help me say what we do with that information. Unique now to homeopathic remedies are mental symptoms.

We now know the mental state for each and every one of the substances that we have as remedies. These people were able to say I'm afraid of death but they felt like they had burning pain but they were restless and anxious. So now what do we do with that information? What medicinal value do these mental symptoms have? They now allow us to use the remedies with much more width and breath than we do with things like an aspirin. We can now give them to people who have had chemotherapy who have taken a known poison under the pretense that they're going to die and are afraid of death.

They're sick and throwing up and have burning pain. We can give them relief with a substance made from arsenic one part per million one part per billion. The more we dilute these remedies the stronger they act. So we can use these super diluted substances and affect people both mentally and physically. We can give them relief of their disease in multiple planes. Now we can also use this information to do acutes. So we can use it for something casual or we can use it for something that has deep pathology.

Part 3: Introduction to Homeopathy

So, Hahnemann went on to prove a lot of remedies. They proved BellaDonna diluted down that mercury to see what else they could do with it that they could actually get rid of infections and that they could get rid of symptoms of senility even with things like mercury. So, Hahnemann's success was well known very quickly. The epidemics of the day were treated successfully with homeopathy. Now what Hahnemann did, in the meantime, was actually made or what we know was our first inoculations. If you wanted to prevent something like cholera or you wanted to do prevention from malaria or the flu he could make a remedy by super diluting the substances of the disease themselves.

They were the first immunizations they were so highly successful that there are still statues today to Hahnemann in Washington D.C. for what he did, well what Homeopathy did, because he's passed on by then. But what Homeopathy did for the population in saving so many more people than were treated with conventional medicine. So what happened in his day in his lifetime at the end of the 1700s hundreds now early 1900s is homeopathy became popular really fast. Who had health care in the late 1700s? The rich. K. So the family in England became patrons of homeopathy. They still have a homeopath as their primary care provider today.

So as the rich began to seek out the Hahnemann and his staff and other doctors that were converting their thinking along with him to doing this practice of using ultra diluted substances to do prevention as well as treatment. It was nontoxic, it was highly effective and there were no side effects. The speed at which the remedies worked were phenomenal. Now as a result of that the politics of the day, and you're up into the 1700s, was exploration if not occupations of countries all over the world. So homeopathy was taken by the French and the English to Africa to India to the United States to South America and Mexico and all over the world. So Homeopathy has been used in these countries including this one since the end of the 1700s.

Now in the United States the first medical college in our country was homeopathic. It still stands in Philadelphia today and it is called the Hahnemann College of Medicine. It has since, in the 1900s, been taken over by the A.M.A. The first research hospitals in the United States were homeopathic and homeopathy was well known and highly effective. You could see a homeopathic physician at the rate of about 50 percent. If you wanted to see a conventional doctor you could but if you want to see a homeopath there were commonly available. There were homeopathic specialists here that did gynecology and dentistry and ophthalmology. The homeopathic books and all the clinical information has been stuffed in rat holes in these hospitals that are currently for the last 20, 30 years being dug back out.

But homeopathy was very popular here and very effective. Now what happened to homeopathy and how come you haven't heard of it. The beginnings of our country's laws are beginning to be passed by Congress and the A.M.A.

actually is from the business point of view is probably a lot more progressive than the homeopaths were. They went to Congress and they passed legislation that said cancer couldn't be treated by anything other than an AMA provider. So cancer is actually only serviced only by the A.M.A. here. You can only treat it with chemo or surgery and radiation. You cannot treat cancer in the United States. All the cancer clinics despite their validity and their success were closed down. If you want to treat cancer today in an alternative way you have to leave the country.

The clinics moved over to Mexico or you have to go to Europe or there are some Canadian clinics as well. But we can't legally treat cancer in the United States. And the next thing that happened is that they took dominion over the words treat, medicate, and prescribe. We can't use those either. In the alternative field we can recommend and we can give you advice but we can't diagnose, treat, or medicate or mess with your medicines. So what happens is the age also the industrial revolution created this environment of us thinking and what we consider to be a very physical or scientific way. What Hahnemann taught us is that the reason that these remedies work in super dilutions is that we're actually getting the remedy to go to our life force.

Our vital force is what animates a body. They all have flesh and they all have. You know you could have just eaten dinner. The difference between somebody alive and dead is whether they have a vital force or they don't. Now the remedies in these super dilutions actually have an effect on that vital force. The balancing and the motivating agents of our bodies. So that wasn't necessarily a popular opinion of the day and it certainly wasn't very popular when the industrial revolution here in the United States was big. We're trying to do everything from our physical understanding and the tools begin to arrive. We now have microscopes. They can look at disease in that microscope, they can see bacteria and viruses and they put a homeopathic remedy in a super dilution one part per billion or smaller so they couldn't see it.

So they accused homeopaths of using placebo despite the fact that the results were outstanding. People were happy doing homeopathy. The effects were obvious and well documented. In the meantime the FDA is formed and all homeopathic remedies still today are FDA approved. The homeopathic remedies were the original United States pharmacy. They still are today. There's never been a recall ever of a homeopathic remedy. And that creates some level of competition. At the same time that these laws are being passed we passed patent laws. Now the patent laws and the reason this is significant is it changes medicine as we know it. Instead of using natural substances which are not patentable because the patent laws say that to all or to possess a patent you have to do something unique.

It can't be something that already exists. You have to develop something new. So if we have arsenic already and calcium and magnesium already exist and chamomile already exists comfrey for those of you who use those herbs. You can't own them. So what the pharmaceutical companies did is actually to make them unique as they studied now that they have those microscopes identifying the active ingredient in a substance. So if we can identify what is an anti-inflammatory about white willow bark then we synthesize it then we sell it back to you as aspirin. So drugs are patented. The pharmaceutical companies own them. That's why the prices are what they are. They can charge whatever people are willing to pay.

In a homeopathic remedy because they're natural substances there are no patents. You can still buy a remedy at the Mart stores or the health food stores or even from us as homeopaths for commonly 10 bucks. So you're not paying for that research and development. Ours is already done. We know what each and every one of these substances does mentally and physically but they're not patentable. So what happens now as a result of that is that it becomes a business to sell medicine. Now to make medicine into a business takes some partners and it takes some thought.

So if we're going to make some business alliances here, what we're going to do is we're going to have you go to the doctor and you are going to tell the doctor that you are all achy and have pains all over your body, that you're having difficulty sleeping and that you're miserable. So they say aha that's called fibromyalgia. So then what they do is the insurance companies step in as a partner and they give it a code and they're only going to pay for a designated treatment. The pharmaceutical partner says OK here's the way it's going to go. You're going to get that muscle relaxer, a pain reliever, some Ambien so that you can sleep and an antidepressant.

Now this is going to come in a box nowadays and that's called the standard of care.

The insurance will only pay for this product provided by only this guy. So they become business partners in medicine. Now while they're looking at this homeopathic remedy under the microscope and can't see it they bashed the tar out of it and create campaigns in the United States to bash all other providers that aren't part of this group. So they didn't pay for chiropractors they did things like call them quacks and how they shamed homeopaths into using whatever those was stupid little sugar pills like placebo even though they worked, even though effective even the homeopaths of the day had trouble defending what the heck was on those and how to get it across. Because we didn't have this money source here.

So what happened is homeopathy really dwindled in the US between 1920s really and 1960s and in 1960 everything changed. In the 60s we now have common flights over to Europe. We've got transportation if you go over to Europe for the young people who went to school there. If they went into the local pharmacy they could buy something like , which is a remedy made for the flu. It's the most effective prevention in the world for the flu. And also treatment in these little local pharmacies and markets that they can buy homeopathic remedies or were recommended and begin to get some experience and bring them back. At the same time that that's taking place, the MRI comes on the scene.

Now once they have an MRI which does magnetic imaging, they put the remedies in the machine and they can see it. They can see that the remedies not only had action in some kind of way that they could measure some kind of what could be known as the frequency that they could see the difference in the potency of something being low potency versus high potency. They could tell the difference between the substances and homeopathy took off. Now in the United States today the medicines that are available or the forms of medicine are wide open. You can see the kahuna healer. You can go to the acupuncturist or the naturopath or the crazy homeopath and get some alternative forms of treatment. We've been validated.

They can map and see these acupuncture points. They can actually measure through that MRI what's happening after, or during, those types of treatment. So we've been validated by the technology and the more technology we have today the more valid homeopathy becomes because as the equipment gets more and more refined the evidence gets more and more, like I said measurable. Over and above the fact that the people get great results. I mean that's the biggest but the homeopathy today and that the circle of alternative medicine that's available to you has now overtaken in popularity what the A.M.A. is providing. When I started this in the 80s the late 80s the stats showed that 78 percent of the American population were seeking regular A.M.A.

provided care. In the year 2000 and went to 50/50. These years after 2010 were over. So it's really a significant thing that people are not happy with the results they're getting with traditional medicine or conventional medicine. They want some other choices and the reason I'm teaching it to you is because there are options. Homeopathic remedies, as a category, are highly effective FDA approved medicinal substances that can give you relief from both acute and chronic diseases. we have in effect the uniqueness that we're going to use remedies instead of drugs or herbs. And the difference between drugs or herbs and having just a diet alone is that there's substances you swallow.

You're going to dissolve them in your belly. You may or may not assimilate them if you take calcium and you have osteoporosis, it doesn't cure the osteoporosis. You may or may not even use the calcium you put in your belly. When we use a homeopathic remedy they go under our tongue or in a mucous membrane we can put them in your eyes we can put them on your skin. We can put them for the cows in the dairies on their vulva. We can put spirits of the animals in their faces where they have any kind of moisture like in their eyes and nose. So homeopathic remedies actually in those mucous membranes have a totally different action. They go to your brain, they go to your nervous system, they go to the origin of the vital force.

Then they tell it to move. If the vital force recognizes the message like, like if your brain was your battery if it has a charge it will respond to the remedy. So it works very much like starting your car. If it's sitting outside and it's got tires and gas but it's not moving. It has everything it needs to run but it's not stuck there. So what you do is you turn that key, the key provides the spark, the spark lights the fuel and you get the car moving down the road. And it'll move until you get where you're going or you run out of gas. That's what a remedy does. It actually wakes up and motivates the system to do what it had intentions to do in the first place. It's supposed to digest food, it's supposed to be healthy. It's not supposed to be depressed and full of anxiety and have sores on your body. We want to get rid of that.

We want to motivate the body toward health. The plan is that you have some awareness of what illness o and health is. That we know and have evidence that you do have movement. That it gets rid of pain or gets rid of mucus or gets rid of a staph infection like Mrsa which the poor A.M.A. couldn't touch with a ten foot pole they have no idea how to solve these problems. When they tell you things like you're going to be a diabetic the rest of your life is because they don't know how to fix it. Not because you're stuck. We can motivate the body with remedies. And change your state of health. So the world of homeopathy is humongous. It's a huge field of medicine. The only thing that we can't do is surgery and we don't want to. It'd be really nice to not need to.

And if you need to we're going to send it to the doctor who's good at that. Right. To a surgeon to take care of it. But homeopathy is highly effective in this huge width and breath of medicine. We can do things like they did for me to give me my whole body and my being a tune that fertility was possible. What's impossible in homeopathy is to do birth control. Can't do it. It can't make the body break. It can only make it work. It can make it not function. There are no side effects to homeopathy. We can't cause a miscarriage. It can only fix them. So there are limitations for us or we can't medicate.

We're only going to make an improvement. We're going to facilitate your body to be the best it can be if it comes if your weaknesses come from things like genetic predisposition. We're going to empower it to the best of our ability. That's where herbs and a good diet come from. Let's support that and maintain it. Let's give it the best we can to empower and give people strength and vitality so they can maintain that state of health. But the goal is to create movement. Our plan when we use a remedy is to set an intention to create movement.

If you're here in the space of healthy happy asymptomatic we're not touching you with a ten foot pole. It's a wonderful spot. If you bump out of it after you get that bill and you worry and don't sleep. And it's worrying, I don't sleep, cranky, stomach aches. And then that stomach ache becomes an ulcer and you're not getting along at home and at work you're going to either start taking something over the counter or seeing your doctor or we're going to create some movement here. We're going to move you to another state because it's uncomfortable. So as you use a remedy or have less and less of these symptoms with a plan using classical homeopathy to get to a place of better health.

Part 4: Introduction to Homeopathy

All of us experience our disease pathology differently. It creates a befuddlement because I have 2000 remedies with me in my pharmacy. Which one do you pick? If you go to a health food store they have 50 or 100. What are you going to do? So the reason for teaching in communities like yours is to teach things like how to use the top 50 remedies, what are the keys to them, how do you select a remedy, how to recognize in your children what it is that you're really giving them the remedy for. In the case of a child what's the first symptom of not feeling good? Whiny clingy droopy they're miserable they don't eat. So at that particular point the disease all starts out as a mental problem.

Right. Has mental symptoms. It's followed by snotty throwing up or diarrhea. If you can get the disease when it's only this big we can move them back to balance with little or no effort. If they start to produce mucus and they start to cough. Now we have more work to do. So to move them back toward balance we're going to change their vitality, get rid of the symptoms and improve their health. But always for chronic diseases the mentals come first and if the mentals don't change with the remedy you've missed something. You're not getting the maximum state of improved health. If I gave you something like, or you go to a medical doctor and you get something like acyclovir for herpes.

What's the next medication you're going to be on? Anti-anxiety drugs. Because it puts the ulcer on the inside. So now what happens is that you get frantic or have pain. That's why these poor shingles people are so miserable. They rub the cortisone on their shingles and it flips over and now they're irritated on the inside and they can't get to it. They're in chronic pain. So followed by the fact that they can't sleep any more now they need some kind of sleep medication. Then the anxiety is created. To cure the anxiety we bring the shingles back. Put them back on the skin, the anxiety goes away and then we get the shingles off. This disease that we have today that they call aging or the horror of things like autoimmune diseases in our youth is from over vaccinosis.

We're putting disease in and packing it in at a rate that's obscene. When I was a kid we had five vaccines before I went to kindergarten. The kids today get 22 before the age of two. They're chronically sick, they're not casually sick. They are not doing disease prevention; it's actually undermining the immune system completely. The theory was homeopathic. A little bit of the snake that bit you a little bit like a cure like we didn't get people disease. We gave them an altered diluted essence of disease. That's non toxic. We didn't put polio on their bodies. We gave them a heads up that they don't get polio. The Homeopathic immunizations are in the 90th percentile of effectiveness with no side effects. They do great prevention.

We're not making people sick under the delusion that being sick makes you healthier. And they've been around for the last 200 years. Document document document we have documentation. Why not? You know the only vaccines required by law in the United States are yellow fever if you visit Africa and Gardasil if you live in Texas. No other vaccines are mandated. No. No other vaccines are mandated by law in the United States. It's called intimidation. They want compliance. Why do they want compliance? Why don't you take your child to health care if they want that vaccine certificate? They want it because the person providing the day care is getting reimbursement from the federal government for their food program.

And that's the requirement if you're going to get reimbursed for these children eating ketchup as a vegetable. Then you have to have them vaccinated. You have to have their vaccine card on file. If you went to somebody that fed your children healthy food and didn't get governments up you know supplementation or you wouldn't need it. And when you go to school the constitution allows us the right to raise our child in the way that we're empowered to by God. So you can sign a religious exemption. Right. You can also do this and this is in my opinion is in some of the things that I've done and my own experiences raising my own children.

You can also tell your pediatrician I will consent to the concept of vaccines for my child, as long as you're willing to be liable for it. If you're willing to sign a document that says when my child gets sick or suffers from any chronic effects that you're going to be responsible for, they won't sign that form. OK. That's the end of that. That's how you get a medical exemption. OK. Or that in your family there's histories of chronic diseases like autoimmune diseases like some of the new things like autism seizure disorders. If you don't have some of those in your family I'd be shocked. With a familial history you are qualified for a medical exemption which is permanent. OK. So you just have to be able to know the facts about vaccines.

I also asked them if vaccines are safe why did the Congress dedicate a fund for the side effects and damage from vaccines. Because they know that a percentage of the population is going to get sick and damaged. Now the irony and the politics of that is that they write off a percentage of our children knowing that that is totally and completely the truth. And in my area and that was , you know, kind of a new idea. I homeschooled my girls in the first years of their life. But in going to my community daycare which I did. Then he used it with some frequency. The woman called me on the phone and she said the group of children here in our school and in my daycare have whooping cough. So I need to contact all the parents and let them know.

And the reality is that they're blaming it on a non-vaccinated child. So the non-vaccinated child who had whooping cough gave it to all the vaccinated kids who were supposedly protected. Then they had the teachers at the school take antibiotics because even after being revaccinated which they encouraged the community to do that didn't provide any protection either. So they put them all on antibiotics and blame the homeschool family. So then they said that it was a bad batch. Well there's nobody that's a native at that school in the state of Montana. The kids are from California

Oregon Pennsylvania Kentucky. They didn't all get vaccinated in the same clinic. So that was hogwash too. OK.

So, these campaigns that they have to bash people who are unvaccinated are really bogus. You just have to have some backbone. You have to do some research. There's many books on the history of vaccines. The efficiency of homeopathic immunizations. And you just need to brush up and be prepared. OK. You can choose to be compliant or non-compliant by filling out your piece of paper with multiple forms that are available to you. But it's always under attack because they want compliance. OK it's not that your child has protection, what they want in my opinion is compliance. It's repetition but children's vaccine kits or children's birthing kids or the family kids. All these selections of remedies have all been put together for you.

So the children's vaccines homeopathically include the MMR the diphtheria pertussis and tetanus the chicken pox the generic antidote to the ill effects of vaccines which produces huge amounts of mucus and allergies in our children. So selections, oh, Hepatitis B is also included in that group of remedies. So they're available to you. Yes. I didn't do the research and my kids were all immunized. Ultimately you can individually and not immunize them by taking away the ill effects but at the same time you're going to protect them with the homeopathic vaccine so you can do them in duel. You can antidote the ill effects in the body. Now what's happened to the children's diseases and the results of these immunizations is that we've mutated diseases into new forms.

So we're calling diseases now by new names. We've renamed things that are commonly known. What's MS? It has the same symptoms as polio with a slow onset. It's mutated. So in children that have hearing problems and recurrent ear infections from the measles vaccine the measles mumps vaccines are alive. What's the mumps? It's a glandular disorder, yes an infection. So now what we have is swollen glands someplace else chronic limp enlargements with huge tonsils. So the diseases have just been moved. We call them by other names who we never heard of when we were kids of RSV? What happened to arteriosclerosis it's now coronary artery disease.

Every 10 years as they reassess the liability of these drugs, they come out with new ones and the diseases evolve into new names and new manifestations. The truth is in the vaccine class that I teach, it takes a good three hours to get through that class to learn the manifestations of these diseases. But we've taken something like a staph infection and because of antibiotics we've moved it into all these different kinds of infections that have different names now. So we've done the same thing with the diseases our children are vaccinated for and we have threats that are really scary. What's an autoimmune disease? Where the immune system is actually so overwhelmed it's not functioning properly. It's broken down.

If the origin of these autoimmune diseases one of the main categories of the origin of that disease is vaccinosis. The vitality diminished because the disease side is stacked up. We're going to put all these drugs and diseases in the body and this vitality goes down as a result. When it breaks down when you bump that 60/40 mark or 50/50 mark it breaks. It can't handle it anymore. It's going to convert this into malfunction. So the goal is to minimize the amount of diseases we put in our body. Now when you go to the market and some child has slobbered on the handle that you've got to push your shopping cart with that recycled air for which staff strep things like spinal meningitis are airborne, are they protected from disease by having these vaccines? If you get on an airplane and somebody is hacking, coughing, choking, etc.

there. Are you protected from those diseases? So what. How is it that you either get sick or don't get sick. It's a direct result of where you are on here because diseases are ever present. When you go to get a sandwich and the person goes like this when they're wrapping it up or putting your mayonnaise on. Are you being protected from disease? Or the fact that they didn't wash the dishes well enough for you in the last 400 people who use the silverware are leaving some germs behind for you. How are you going to protect yourself? You can't isolate yourself and you really can't avoid being exposed. How your immune system works is to be at its maximum or top functioning. So all of us that do alternative medicine are looking to improve that vitality. We want evidence.

We want to know that instead of you being at a 2 vitality when you get out of bed in the morning that we could achieve four five six seven. Right, Great. We want to feel great. We don't want to be snotty. We don't want to be always wearing mini pads. How many women? If you go under the market how many square feet are dedicated to something you have to put between your legs because you're dripping. So it's really obscene. How many adults have sinus infections or chronic dripping of their nose? They're sick all the time. We just call that normal. Right. (I know someone that's had allergies her entire life, she's only 25, and now she's developed symptoms of MS) What that is is it's a weakened immune system right.

And whatever her genetic predisposition and her imprints are that allow her to have weaknesses and strengths her weaknesses are going to be in her nervous system. And we know by the combination, I know by the combination of those two that it's kidney related. OK. So kidneys are for which the nervous system is regulated from or influenced by. So MR is the nervous system and allergies are kidney. So they're highly related diseases or the origin is related. You can undo disease based upon the person's vitality, the level of suppression and how willing they are to you know to do what we call classical treatment which is to treat the totality.

It's really difficult to undo the disease process with acute remedies or substances. You can't cure MS with herbs either, if you put them in your belly. You have to go after the origin of disease and respect the totality that you're treating. So people like classical acupuncturists or classical homeopaths have that mentality: what's the totality of what's happening here and how do I shift as a working unit? OK, how do I undo this disease process? So that's considered what we call classical thinking is Totality. We can teach you to do remedies for your family without creating suppressions by fixing bug bites and injuries and cuts and trying not to burn. You can do those things inexpensively and painlessly with great results.

How to stop bloody noses which is really a chronic problem not an acute one is why would you have the tendency to spring a leak. Later later in life, the people who spontaneously bleed, what about later in life having hemorrhoids or the blood clots. I mean they're real. It's a sign of a problem. It's just considered to be small in their youth but it is telling you and warning you of signs of having a weak circulatory system. So there's more to this story. There's more meaning to these symptoms when they're accumulated and looked at from the big view instead of symptom by symptom. (So how do you learn to diagnose that yourself, as a layperson who doesn't have all the information you do? You don't. First of all we can't treat, diagnose or prescribe so we can't do that at all.

So what we're going to do instead is we're going to take an assessment of your symptoms and then make a decision based upon your history and your current symptomatology. If you happen to have access or bring things like lab tests or let's say that you've been told that you have a cyst or a tumor of x size then by using the remedies we want to see that your overall well-being improves that your symptoms diminish and you can use your doctor to monitor the size of that tumor to make sure system make sure it's shrinking. So the tools are not incompatible. Well it's incompatible with the treatment.

If we're going to cover up or suppress a problem instead of resolve it, that's where we have conflict. Now Hahnemann when he came up with these homeopathic principles did some politically incorrect things. What he said is that if you cover up a disease manifestation only to make the body sicker later, that's not healthy and that's not what doctors should be doing. So ultimately he made a huge field of enemies because anybody practicing medicine who uses drugs that suppresses a problem then is according to Hahnemann is doing bad work. So what I'd like to say is that that unpopular opinion that MDs don't want to own is the fact that when you ask for help your bladder is leaking and you take a drug for it to stop the battery problem, what results next is additional kidney issues or kidney disease or more chronic problems.

It's beside the point because he gave you what you asked for. You asked for relief. His intentions weren't to hurt you. His intentions were to give you relief of what you complained about. If you go in and have pain and they give you a pain reliever, the fact that you get constipated or lethargic or can't get out of bed the next morning or can't operate machinery at work for the next three days because you're drugged is beside the point. You asked for pain relief. So what we do in homeopathy is resolve the pain without the side effect. How about if we get rid of the pain and you can operate machinery and don't have constipation.

Their intention isn't necessarily bad. The result is bad and what he was trying to do is educate and separate out what the origins of disease. Where is disease coming from, how do we resolve it? His intention wasn't to bash the A.M.A. or the medical doctors of the day. It was to educate them that there is more to disease and there's consequences and there's a new tool that we can use to not create a suppression. So the AMA and homeopaths have been split from the very beginning because of it.

Part 5: Introduction to Homeopathy

Yes. (I've heard of arnica. What's the difference between that and Tiger's balm?) Tiger Balm, products that carry things like or contain things like camphor menthol eucalyptus tea tree oil are aromatic substances that are actually bronchodilators. The reason that we want to rub Vicks vapor rub on our feet or on our chest is that they open up your breathing tubes. OK. So they are medicinal substances in their own right but they're incompatible with homeopathy. They won't work together. Now the difference between you rubbing that aromatic tiger balm on your arthritis is that it doesn't resolve the arthritis. You have to rub it on there multiple times a day like you would take an aspirin. So it gives you relief that way it's temporary.

If you used a high enough potency of arnica you could get relief that has great longevity and start to resolve the inflammation and it doesn't smell bad either. (Well like when your husband showed up to that guy, you know and saw the shingles, Yes. That was quick... he didn't ask all the questions that he asked you?) Oh, he asked him 10 questions to figure out which remedy he was going to use for the shingles. but it was a 10 minute consultation instead of a two hour consultation because he treated it as acute. He didn't treat it as a chronic disease. What I had was completely different. What I had is why is my body not functioning properly.

So let's see what it's going to take to clean out any old junk and create a tuneup. (Because the shingles were showing up as something acute So he was still trying to find out what is the problem with why this person is having the shingles?) He didn't attend that appointment and they never came back. But remember the remedies have mental and physical symptoms. So let's say that he had anxiety for some reason that led to him having that outbreak. So whatever remedy he used quelled the anxiety so he didn't get shingles back. (Right. Your husband might have placed himself in that stressful situation?) Not necessarily because we open the mail every day. OK. So what happens when we use a remedy that changes the chronicity of disease it changes our perception.

So when the mail comes you say one more piece of mail and I'm going to jump versus oh ok I guess I'm going to make payments. There's a difference in where you're at in this scale of disease. It doesn't keep the mail from coming in, it doesn't mean he's not going to be in a stressful environment. How many here have more than two kids? Does that change? No. Whether you yell scream flip out kick then you know throw things is where you're at on this scale. If you say hey let's everybody sit down and we'll all do 10 minutes to get this taken care of or on this side you go you know you scream and get everybody in the yard while you're cursing and slamming and banging in the you know unloading the dishwasher. It's different how we solve the problem.

But the problem's the same, the motivation for the problem is still there. The instigator of the problem. (Right the problem is our progression if it isn't taken care of, possibility.) Well what happens is that you can stay in the same state over and over and over and over and over. Where you get in trouble is when you start medicating. If you take a high blood pressure drug. So here's what people say to me. I said, " What can I do for you?" What brought you here. They say well I just had my annual checkup. I went to the doctor and the doctor asked me how I was doing. I said you know I'm having trouble breathing a little breathless. And the doctor says well I did some looking at him and he said you know you have an enlarged heart. He asked, "Why do I have an enlarged heart?"

How'd that happen? He said Well let me look he said you know you've been on high blood pressure medicine for 20 years. You've had high blood pressure for 20 years. So the fella says I don't have high blood pressure. You've been giving me pills for 20 years so I didn't. So the covering up of a smaller problem created a much bigger one. So now what's he going to do? I mean now you've got to deal with that state. And the proof that this stuff happens is that they know what's coming next in a lot of cases. So they can actually put the two meds together. So now we're getting blood pressure pills with a water pill in it. So we're caught we're getting some hydrochlorothiazide with your blood pressure pill. Why do they do that?

Because when your heart begins to be stressed you're going to have congestive heart failure. Ankles are going to start swelling. So how about we just go to put the hydrochlorothiazide right in the blood pressure pill. So it hides the next symptom. Where this becomes a problem is when our elderly or older people go to the doctor or the hospital in the winter. They can't breathe, they can't lie flat in bed, they have anxiety about their state, they're coughing and they start giving them antibiotics as if they have the flu and they don't respond. So what's really happening is the nurse comes in who is trained to look at their ankles and she looks at the ankles and she says there's no swelling. Write it on the report that it's not congestive heart failure.

It's the flu. So they're still non-responsive to the antibiotics you're going to lose them they're in trouble they've gotten pneumonia. So what I tell my patients to do is the family is you go outside in the hallway and you know buy their meds because their meds include hydrochlorothiazide the water pill. So I have them go outside and to the nurses station and tell them this is congestive heart failure. They'll come in, they'll test for it and then they'll put him on something like Lasix and get that water off. But it's not pneumonia. So it creates misdiagnosis because they're medicating the symptoms that would be warning you you're in trouble. Does that make sense? OK. So the diseases get more and more complicated.

And when those complications appear the style in medicine is to medicate the next symptom hence the Tupperware is full of stuff people carrying around with them or those little pill boxes where you can have so many you have to put them all in there for the week so that you can remember which ones to take. So the goal of health is to minimize the need for that. I tell my clients I cannot take you off your meds.

I cannot adjust your medication. The goal is to not need it. How about if you don't have anxiety. How about if you don't have depression. How about if you don't have high blood pressure.

How about if you don't have gout. So we can educate him about dietary things to follow that up and we can also get rid of why they have the disease in the first place. I go to visit my family and I have my homeopathic bag. So I just walk in the door and I live, you know, a plane ride away from my family so I'm not there all the time. When I opened the door my mother said to me, "Do you have anything in that bag that will keep your dad from leaving his shoes in the hallway? And I said I probably have a remedy in here so you won't notice. And when I thought about it for a minute I thought I have to explain myself.

So I said mom you homeopathy is really strange and unique I say depends on how you feel about those shoes. You said if you feel like Dad's been disrespectful to you because you like the house clean and left his shoes there that's one remedy. If you're afraid you're going to trip and fall over those shoes and get hurt, that's another remedy. If you're afraid the neighbors are going to see the house and think less of you, that's a different remedy. So how exactly do you feel about those shoes? And that's how different homeopathy is or how unique it is. So when we talk about things like a migraine which is a medical name for a headache K of a certain type we ask people how do you experience a migraine.

So if your head feels like it's going to explode or somebody else feels like their head is being crushed in a vice while another person feels like they have needles and pins behind their eyes. So the reason for their headaches also differs. One person has financial stress, one has relationship problems and one of them ate too much chocolate. So the reason we give the remedy as well as the way they manifest it is unique to each remedy. So there's hundreds of remedies for headaches. It's why you have a headache. How about we get rid of the fact that you have headaches instead of treating the headache.

So the possibility of thinking just a little bit further is the homeopathic drama right. Is that we're interested in how you feel and how you experience your problem. If you had four children that have a cold or the flu in the house they all have different symptoms. One of the children has sinus infections. The other one may throw up every time they don't feel good. And other kids cough every time the wind blows. So even now we're calling it all the flu we have individually unique ways of manifesting disease. If we had a meeting around the table for all of us who are from those big families. Let's talk about your mother. So we can talk about you know one person says my mother was a saint and the next one said my mother was selfish and she had favorites.

And the other one says that my mom was you know ornery and picked on me. And you wonder what family they all came from. Because we all have our own perceptions and dilemmas both mentally and physically. The uniqueness of homeopathy is that we care about that. It's really similar to what it used to be for an old GP. He knew that your dad was a tyrant and that that ulcer that you have is from stress they'd give you a Valium. Now you have to go to a doctor for your heart and one for your feet. And a gynecologist and a podiatrist and you know it just keeps on going. So the further they take our bodies apart the smaller they look at it as our DNA, or as do we secrete serotonin. The more that happens the higher the side effects.

If you stand back and look at somebody in totality, what's the dilemma, what's the consequences that this person is dealing with, and shift that, then we can resolve and improve their overall well-being, not just the headache. Does it make sense? So it's possible and homeopathy is infinite. We can learn to do acutes. That's the beginning and the reason it is easier to learn than anything else is because we all experience them the same. If we want to do an experiment and we all want to slam our finger on this car door right, or this big wood door. What would happen? We'd all have the same sensation. It takes your breath away, you're probably wanting to cry and your finger starts to throb.

You are worried that your nail might fall off. You know your fingers are going to turn blue and you're stuck in the air while you're thinking about it. So what happens is that we can divide the way we treat that for a double blind. We can give a third of you some pain reliever like a Tylenol and you can take that every four hours but you're still going to turn blue and fall off. You probably have trouble getting your jeans on for three or four days. We can take that other thing and give you the homeopathic remedy hypericum like you use it every five minutes three times in a row every hour three times and you're good to go. It doesn't turn blue. Your neck won't fall off and you forget about it the next day. The third group is going to use placebos.

Those poor guys are going to suffer. Your finger's going to throb like heck, you're going to sneak some Tylenol, k. Because it is ineffective. So what we want to do is recognize that everybody in acute for the most part has the same circumstance. If you burned yourself on the wood stove, you got that big blister on your palm. Everybody experiences it the same. It's going to turn white, the flesh dies, you're going to get a blister. If we can rub calendula on that homeopathically or burn crame the pain goes away. It doesn't form a blister and you know it's gone in a day or two after three or four applications you don't have to be miserable. That's acute. We all experience that situation in a similar way. So now we can use the same remedy in these kits that we make for family kids.

The remedies in here are tools for acutes. So you can pick the remedy for slamming your finger in the car door, you can pick the remedy for a burn, you can pick the remedy for a bug bite and get results for all children in the family in the neighborhood. When we're doing chronic disease like fixing my hormones or how about you resolve my insomnia then we need to know what's personal about you that is in that dilemma. OK what's unique to you. Then we'll pick the remedy. And then we'll move out of the way while you're doing that whether that be stress or whether that be you know your personal dilemma. So these tool boxes are huge.

And the reason that we use them and encourage you to have them is you can't do any harm with homeopathy.

It's safe, it's nontoxic if you pick the wrong remedy that doesn't work. If you pick the right remedy you get results you only repeat it until you resolve the problem and then you're done. So if that's 10 minutes or you know three days. When you're done you're done. We don't ongoingly medicate. We try to solve the problem. Homeopathic remedies packaged properly don't have expiration dates; they last forever. The only contaminant to remedies is camphor menthol eucalyptus and I profess that tea tree oil is in that category. Things like oil or oregano if you're really into essential oils, the pungent trees you want to avoid. Things like peppermint that some of these companies really encourage you to use.

They don't tell you the whole story. If you're using peppermint for digestion it causes the sphincters to relax so it increases regurgitating your food. So if you have reflux it makes it worse. It might help the digestion but it doesn't help the regurgitating. So there's more to the story when we medicate with herbs or medicinal substances and knowing the whole story sometimes gives you a much better use of it. Things are not just good for this or good for that. They have side effects or they have you know reasons that they are acting the way they do. So that's why classes are so significant. So homeopathy is a huge field of medicine. We can do many things with it. Tomorrow I'm going to teach a class called the Family Class and what we're going to do there is we have six hours to learn the top 50 remedies.

It's hot and fast we're going to learn what it is that's medicinal about each substance. We're not going to learn everything that's in a book. Homeopathy is the most documented form of medicine that we have available in the world. We know the mental and physical and the pathology and the clinical indications for every remedy. What we want to do is figure out how to do that fast. You slam your finger in the car door, you grab the woodstove and have a big nasty burn on your hand. You want relief right now. So if we learn which remedy is for burns on which remedy is for the bloody nose or which remedy is for slamming your finger in the car door you're going to be able to pick it just like that. So we're going to learn that that's the Family Class.

The other classes that we have available would be alternative immunization classes and learning about the diseases and how to re immunize or not immunize your children from their traditional vaccines. We teach veterinary classes. How to use the remedies for your animals, whether that be dairy or livestock or your pets. I teach an ongoing theory class in multiple communities so that you can learn how to use the books and the resources and start asking why questions and getting the answers to those questions what is genetic predisposition What do I do with it if that runs in my family how am I going to handle or deal with it how do I stay out of that vulnerability to actually manifest it.

You can have a genetic predisposition doesn't mean you have to get sick. So teaching in those theory classes more and more and more about chronic diseases. I have a class where we teach the next 40 remedies after the family class and that class will be talking a lot more about behavior disorders and things like jealousy and ADHD. Elements like autism and how to assess those cases to be able to make certain better remedy selections on a more chronic basis instead of so acutely. So there's lots of information I'm willing to share with you. I just need the interest of the community and I'll provide it for you. And I thank you for coming.

Cyber Security Threat Intelligence Researcher

All right. So now you've gone through the intro part. Welcome to the first Book. This is the cyber threat intelligence research certification. This certification is for everybody who wants to get more into information security roles and especially your intelligence roles as part of the cybersecurity workforce. So I will try to make this certificate as easy when it comes down to explaining as many concepts. And then Of course when we go into different phases when it comes to sort of Akkad we'll have some labs and I will also make you more familiar with some new concepts and some concepts that you already would be familiar with in the past. OK. All right.

So let's roll on to start with the full certificate of dividing it into many Books and this particular Book is the first Book it's called the different phases of threat intelligence. So I have divided this into smaller chapters or smaller classes around seven to eight classes so that you can easily understand and learn on the go or can zoom whatever I am teaching you and to try to also make some real time use of that also. As we go into the Books a little bit more deep I would say you would need to follow a lot of labs and also to do your own research work ethically Of course remember that. All right. So moving on. So what is cyber threat intelligence so that is the question you know which comes to everybody's mind

Of course. You have gone through certain chapters and you know that there is ethical hacking.

You know there is ATP that is like threat intelligence. You know it is like reverse engineering. Actually it is not. Right. So then we talk about threat intelligence or cyber intelligence. We have to understand that the concept goes much beyond or deep from a list of IP addresses. But the poor reputation I would say are hashes which are suspected of bad files. So it is beyond that. So intelligence is not just looking into those IP addresses, those different hashes like some bad malware or axes or you know deloused and so forth. Right. So CGI is evidence based knowledge if you know either an emerging or an existing threat. All right. And that can be used. So this knowledge you gather while steading of a trade which is already there is something which is new. OK.

And this knowledge then you take with you to make some informed decisions and let your management know also and you as a member of the intelligence team should also know how to respond to these different decisions in different ways you know threats which it's hard to get faced with. So SETI encompasses that and also CDI provides more than just specific bits or bytes of that threat. I would say it also provides the context around it. Who the attackers are, where that came from.

Things of that sort. Right. And you will come to know a few concepts around like how to identify the indicators of the attack how how you see the indicators of the compromise you know what are those different indicators you'd come to know and you would be aware of those when you are going to get deeper into different concepts within the class Of course and potentially even the identity and the motivation of the attacker. So I'll teach you how you can identify yes you can dig down and find out what motivation piece is basically putting all the puzzle together. Right. And in the security industry in the security field you will hear these terms a lot.

Phases Overview Part 1

So skilled practitioners and security technology itself by technology means you or your software which you have implied that you're deployed and you or your organization so they can use CGI to better protect against threats or even to detect the existence of threats within a trusted environment. I would say that exceptions are high that CGI will significantly improve system or network security when it is integrated with organizations infrastructure and its operations. I would say so too. Intelligence will not improve anything unless you are using it correctly. You are stedding the knowledge, taking it back and analyzing it to a point right. So by using CGI security teams usually look not to stop each attack as it happens but to also get a better sense of who is attacking what the different methods are different techniques and what are the different targets.

You know it all. You come to understand and know when you are looking for different parts of CGI. So saboteur intelligence is the key to gaining that level of understanding about a particular cyber threat or a predator cyber attack. All right. Let me actually give you a little example to understand this and how companies have used it in the past right. So if you look at the chapter this is a good example where Microsoft actually teamed up with the FBI to take down a botnet which is a very active botnet and it was called The Game over Zeus botnet right. So those of you who were in the security field must have heard about it and this is the game of war where a company a big profile company like

Microsoft went out and their role was that they're taking to do their take like technical actions and conducting and analyzing also this peer to peer network which was basically the game of where it was bottlenecked. Right.

Also true and this monitoring was happening through and it does additional feed from you know maybe a shadow server was put in place and Microsoft was actually able to do some augmentation there and have a bit more visibility into the numbers a number of impacted IPs that you know identify the cyber attack intelligence program and also identify you know who are trying to identify the cyber threat vectors and also identify what the computers are getting and are basically hampered by this.

So these kinds of scenarios happen a lot actually in the security industry. So a lot of companies will have a good practice of cyber intelligence programs and also have you know good response teams and they work very closely with ISP to help the owners of the compromised computers to regain control of their systems. And this is basically Of course you always have to keep law enforcement into confidence so they know what's going on and you don't step in the wrong arena and you're not you're not you know suspected as one of those bad guys been trying to augment or trying to contain a particular malware.

Phases Overview Part 2

OK so now you understand CDA I've given you an example of how companies use CGI and how they can you know gain trust and then basically Lupin FBI to to catch these culprits. And basically the hackers and the bad guys are right. So now let's move forward and I'm going to actually give you a little bit of insight into this chapter. This is the insight into the full trade intelligence you know techniques you know what you'll be talking about basically several techniques and I'll be going over those techniques and the agenda part this coming forth. All right. So to understand what CGI is in its core process this is like those seven steps and the first one out here is hunting.

So I will actually go a little bit into each one of these and then subsequently I will explain them a little bit more to you so you understand them and you understand how exactly they fit into the big picture. Right. So coming back hunting so before starting any kind of analysis you need to actually give us some simple samples and some simple knowledge of your software about what is going on here. Right. So you need to make and develop those skills. You have to hunt for the software online and hunting is basically as does the word also you know implies that you go there you look for different patterns first you look for the malicious software then only you can try to do anything with that software.

So hunting is the first step I would say. Then comes the order of features and behavior and extraction. So once you have gone and done your hunting part now you have to see what the features are. And these are the static features mind you but you need to extract. And same goes to the behavior. So the behavior part when it comes to the feature extraction behavior is basically once you have a good idea when you've done some hunting and you've extracted some basic features out of using your feature and extraction phase then you go and look at the behavior of that particular malware. Right. And basically you will need to know what is going on when it comes down.

What does it do when you download it from the Internet? Is it an algorithm to steal or to hide or to launch some other files or is it opening a backdoor to do that or like the kind of behavior malware would do? This Of course has much more to it. Right. So that is what behavior literally means moving forward clustering and correlation is the next I would say step and which after hunting after you're done Feagin behavior you need to basically take that and start clustering it into groups. Why? Because these groups then will help you better understand what a top floor is. So remember you are a threat intelligence researcher. You have to identify all these different malwares and softwares and any other malicious file that you get you are studying. You have to identify.

You have to identify it piece by piece feature by feature and separate them out. All right. Dentally you can do a full analysis on that particular malware. Right. So mainly You should know some pieces which you should know around here. What are the actor attributes right? Mainly after you've done your clustering now that draped tricked actor attributes is also a key thing that you should know. So that is like who is the doctor who is the perpetrator who is behind the whole operation. Right. That is something that everybody wants to know. Your boss will say "Where is this coming from and who's attacking us or who's locked down our file?" So that's the time you need to wear your researcher hat and then try to get the right information out.

So to identify the right doctor it is important to know that you know who is doing it Of course but then also the way it is then where is it coming from where is the command and control. So if there is any right to see and see where and when it is launching the control of the victim machine or the different differences you know I would say things are part of that. Right. Next thing is tracking and taking down. So once you've identified the piece you know pieces of it like you know these are the different features of the behavior dissolves are clustered there.

They are correlated. Now you have to basically track it down to its source right and take it down. That is the final step and taking down again is basically sometimes coming down. You have to physically work with the local law enforcement and even international law enforcement like Europol or even if they're in other parts of the world to work with them and get the bad guys down. Of course working with the law enforcement gives them all the evidence which you have.

Phases Overview Part 3

Next one thing which I want to make sure of is that you understand all the different steps which I'm going through. So these will help you. This will help you design the full class which basically is around all these different steps. All right. So now let's look at trade intelligence research goals. What are the different goals when it comes down to trade intelligence research? All right. So the first one is to identify and track trade actors. Well that's one of the goals at the end of every research you should know and you should be able to locate and track who has basically conducted that attack. You should also be able to help to be proactive instead of reactive.

And that's one thing that you should know when coming into the security field is that you know you have to be proactive when it comes down to anything you write from hunting to you know getting samples going all the way. And even collaborating with other security engineers and other security. Now I will say researchers online even collaborate with reverse engineers to understand malware better. So that is something which you know that you'll come to Of course you will come to know with experience and that those are very important traits when it comes down to it. I would say for the church intelligence researcher right.

Also broader detection is another thing that you should look at is by finding more and more malware from you know different parts of different segments of the Internet. I would say so. The other thing is that once you have once you know certain traits of a malware you should have a full picture of that attack. That is super important to make any kind of decision. So your discoveries when it comes down to the malware the pieces you know you have to kind of put everything together work with different teams even go above and beyond. And you know in all other companies even if it's competition when it comes to companies you'd be surprised they know how. Of course in the zero day everybody wants to protect it and put their stamp on it.

But if it's not then it will help you especially like you know. And if they have some certain experience in IT in a different strand or different I would say a copy of that malware which you are fighting against or trying to protect against. All right. And another thing is discovering the insights of malware is key. And for example if you're connected to if the malware is what it does you know like behavior it's usually what happens is some malware. As soon as they download, they connect to the Internet. Right. So malwares start extracting files and cleaning and deleting files you know are going forward.

The credentials on the infected machine. Like I mean the admin credentials right. C Judaism the behavior is what you should look at but it comes down to intelligence researchers especially when you're trying to classify trying to understand you know what what traits when you're looking at and the difference. And as a certain diligent researcher some goals that you should always keep as part of your I would say agenda whenever you're looking at something is basically is it is it. Does it stand out? Is it suspicious? Like how you should start analyzing it. Right.

So do some of the traits you will build over time as the CGI skill set. And also you should know when you were what you ever do when you're trying to get information about an infiltration the techniques which you should be using. And Of course you know who is responsible for the full operation. So you're able to understand the full picture by knowing piecing up all the different parts of the puzzle. Right. So all these different Mauer's you know which are out there it could be you know there's a single person or there could be a group of people you know a gang you know. So. So a gang dismantled can happen if you work with Of course I said local authorities law enforcement Interpol Europol FBI and so forth.

Right. So even international organizations always pitch in to help the bad help you catch the bad guys and because they are facing the similar same kind of threats in their countries also. So good good things to remember always work with the law enforcement and always try to build the whole puzzle. Be proactive. All right. Great. So this kind of brings us to the end of class one. And in class actually I'll get a bit more into hunting which is a good trick to stick to start with. And it comes down to trade intelligence researchers. All right thanks for joining us in class too.

Hunting Part 1

We'll come back. This class offers the first Book, which is cyber threat intelligence research certification. And I'm going over different phases when it comes down to several of intelligence right. So look at this pretty picture here. So these are all the different phases or techniques you know you might say these are different phases and I'm going to go with the first one that is hunting in the prayer class. I did go over all of them one by one and just to make you familiar with it. So these words don't sound or whatever I'm explaining doesn't go doesn't sound too new to you. Right. All right. So there's a few classes which I want you to pay special attention to.

And the first one, hunting , is a very interesting class for me and it should be for you also because this is where everything starts. All right. Let's move forward. So what is the goal behind hunting? So I want you to understand the goal to start hunting is basically a technique which is used to collect samples from different sources and different threat sources and in turn these samples they help you to start profiling this malicious malicious software or even malicious actors behind these softwares. So we need to gather these samples from all these different sources which are what you can get your hands on so you can identify all of them. And this all encompasses and is part of hunting. All right, the first month sounds very simple.

Just get there and just gather samples from different sources and then you try to make sense of it. But hunting is how you do that. Right. It's not that you're just going on and on and on like the Internet and you just type in something and empty five hashes and it'll start giving you data. Right. It's not that simple either. Right. That's where you have this class. Now explain it to you. And that's why you play. Pay special attention to how we classify these sources and how you get hold of different permission from different places and piece it all together. All right. So let's move forward. So again now. First thing is if you look at different sources and I want you to be familiar with the term virtual. You will keep on hearing that as VirusTotal. All right, giving you a little background on VirusTotal. The Website is VirusTotal dot com. It has been there for over ten years now.

And it's a web based tool. And why this total is basically now part of Google Google thinks so acquired it. It was a free service and a lot of the software is FREE still you can go in and analyze files you're enabling. You can do the invocation of waitress's bombs Trojans all different kinds of malicious content. And these all can be detected through or actually searched for two hours total. And the main thing in VirusTotal is it is basically it. It kind of works with all the different anti-virus engines and website scanners which look out for all these different tricks out there. Right. So why still blue simply acts as an information aggregator.

I would say it's the only cool one which you would use in order as they are certain they don't research a lot actually. And that this aggregated data basically is the output of your different anti-virus is also the up side scanners in files. And your last analysis tools. So the you're l analysis tools that are there which will basically also go in and tell you which IPs on your bills are how they are. So they all gather this data. And even users go log and contribute to why that's total. That's why it has the back off all these different keys no antivirus is out there and also users have started submitting data to it.

And you can imagine 10 years growing very intelligent just because of some of the damage it has and VirusTotal not only tells you whether a given antivirus solution detected a submitted file but also displays the exact detection label returned by each engine. So it has got that classification that you know and I'll show you how it basically shows that information also in the coming classes and the coming sleights. Well it's another thing a very useful service which VirusTotal offers is the hunting or the intelligence on intelligence solution from Bristol. All right.

So this is a service that is a paid service and that what it does is it also lets you Of course lets you search everything and also lets you download samples of those files from their database so that way you always know what is going on you can also while doing these searches you can apply your own rules and we can be talking about the rules and what they are and how they work. But basically just some rules which you can run on Vitas total and it gives you good information back. And these rules Of course. OK you can automate a lot of stuff using their API also involved with wireless total and all this can automatically get emailed to you back itself. So pretty interesting overall what a tool and even the paid part of it is well worth it.

Hunting Part 2

All right. So next thing after total is understanding go off underground hacking forums. So the underground hacking forums basically let you go and search for a lot of these militias. I would say code which is lying is there malicious malware which is out there and on these phones people are discussing this. We can even find you know certain downloads of malwares. Though personally I think it's a little risky business when it comes down to engaging actively with these forums. So I would propose some caution down there these underground forums where I'm not talking about regular hackers are COM forums and these are like off the radar.

These are like part of you know a different concept not to adhere to and indexed not to your normal indexed file websites. These are the ones which you cannot search on your Googles and being and other search engines. So be very cautious and very aware of what you do and what you download from there. And I would actually highly recommend not to download anything from these forums but I wanted to expose these to that underground hacking forums is one thing where all this happens you know people are interacting and tracking and further and you get into the Book I'll explain to you why you should be cautious and how far you can go when interacting with these kind of forums. All right.

Again Next up is another day another interesting concept is deep web so deep web. The regular reboot you know right now is basically you take your eye to Google or any other popular web browser and go and search for your favorite sites right. But the deep web usually cannot be searched like that. These are the hidden sites and knobbly they are being accessed by power. And Tor is not only another way to access the internet but it is a very secure way in which it literally goes in and tries to search or does a good search on the known index files which are still discoverable and which are not being accessed by normal search engines. All right.

And the Tor browser is there. So it's like an onion browser. That's what's also called. So this browser is good to go and it doesn't. Basically you have no it doesn't. It hides you and it also goes behind a proxy. It sets you up in such a way that your location is also a scrambled little bird if you're sitting in the US . It will show that you're in another part of the world. And so that's how deep the web is, your non-indexed and still searchable part of the Internet which I'll explain is huge and it's actually much bigger than the regular internet which you all guys know about. All right. There's a lot of malicious Saturday habit chaplains out there but hackers they're selling ex-wifes and and müller's so deep web is not something that you just go and just download and start playing with.

No and that's why I'm kind of putting all the red flags to you and you'll understand why they run down in the Book also. But I don't want you to have even Gilbert knowledge getting used to a word called Deep Web and then download your browser and start you know searching for malware and stuff you could get in trouble. So don't do that but do it to understand what it is. First, All right. So next is instant instant response engagement. How does that work? So as a security analyst you will be working for many companies for consultancy services forms instate outstate in the country, even remotely from different countries. Right.

It is very common that you'll be looking through different systems. Mainly those systems that have been compromised because sometimes you're part of a red team and they get you down there to analyze what's going on or even to perform some analysis beforehand right. So humans need to grab a lot of information for sure. And you could gather these from these compromised systems also. And this could be you. You're being guided or told to get some deal files or grab some axes executables and you don't know and they also don't know what it is. Right.

So having to analyze these files you have to send them back to your team sometimes and most times you try to do it first to try to contain it and then send it back once they analyze it they send you information about the piece of the malware. And this is also another way of hunting actually. So you can do some intelligent responsive engagements there and then you basically go and grab some information, send it back for analysis, and get back the information which your core team or our center has provided to you. And then you can basically go and go and you know do some kind of analysis on top of it.

So basically it's more that kind of thing but not but definitely it's another way to gather your malicious samples and to get more feedback and information on it and contain it. Next is another concept which you must have already heard. Honeypots So you're still talking about hunting guys, a few of you who are joining us right now or just want to give some context to hunting and we're just going over different ways in which you can do hunting. All right. So honeypots are a lot you have heard about and traditionally it was actually basically you set up different servers and then you then you make those available you basically take some servers or environment and you expose it on the Internet you open some ports on it. Right.

It's like a honeypot right over you know the honeybee comes. Or any other be comes into it sticks to it. So you could kind of create that environment to track the bad guys. Very simple right. And once you open these ports you know and these bad guys they will come in you will be surprised how fast they go. These guys can reach you out of your environment which you just set up because there are these automated tasks which a lot of these bad guys out there are these hackers that are put in place so even Organization hacking organizations that are put in place. And they look for specific IP addresses. Right. And ports want to see a port opened and they start entering that. So that's all there, that's all you honeypot is set up and that's what the report is right. So you're basically attracting all these hackers and attackers right.

And once they get in then you start gathering samples of the infection. Maybe it was from the port. Maybe it is from.

From a sample this got downloaded. So because it's in a contained environment you kind of control it. Right. So you have to make sure you are contained in my mind and then once they get there then your hunting starts. You start hunting for all the different ways all the different samples that you can get from the doctors and the hackers. All right. OK. So next one is. And this is your open source intelligence. Oh yes I am. So open source intelligence. Basically it is a well known term as you all know. This is basically going on your internet on Google on your popular search engine because we bang anything right and going and searching and hunting for four different parts of information.

So that is another key piece you know where you go in and see what is the public in publicly available information for this particular source. So that's again a different act of hunting. And this is called the O.S. and it's basically stamped open source intelligence gathering. All right. So this actually brings us to the end of class which was basically explaining the phases that are hunting in this case at a very high level. I'll have another full class on hunting. You're not done with hunting and then I'll go a little bit deeper into all these different thousand and you know deep web and different techniques in it which I talked about. All right. Well thanks for joining. I'll see you in the next class and give you that overview view about the next phase that is a feature extraction. Thanks for joining.

Features Extraction Part 1

So a certain diligence researcher you get to know all the different phases when it comes down to your intelligence or CGI. Right. So today I'm going to be talking about a feature extraction which is actually the second phase or second part when it comes to the different techniques for your search. Diligence. Ring So so far we have gone over the first part that was hunting. Right. And we talked about non-malicious binary use of different files. How you kind of know , go and find them. So next is basically the intelligence of when it comes on to your feature extraction. So in this phase you will learn what to do with those samples that you've gone in and fetched or analyzed or downloaded or got access to.

All right. So first things first as far as you know that you know the binary is there with you. Now you've done your hunting part. So next is as I mentioned as sort of intelligence and as you know the words the specified threat intelligence is basically a part of your full phase that is the different seven phases and you know hunting is part of it and even a feature extraction which we are going to talk about right now. Right. So in this phase you will learn what to do with all the samples you collected and how to further analyze them. All right. So is this game on. Now you've got the access to those samples right. So the goal of feature extraction is to identify unique static features in a binary memory static word.

So it basically takes an end feature extraction to identify the unique and static features in a binary that will further help you classify them into specific malicious groups. Right. And that is the main goal behind the high end feature extraction. All right. So what does this literally translate to. Well as a security analyst and intelligence investigator your goal is to get static features like Vicci. For that you don't have to run any piece of code. These are part of your binary. Right. And then you grouped them into different you know buckets. And this is the best way to detect what features belong and to which specific malware group. Right. So then you're going to find which malware groups are involved in that particular threat for that matter. All right.

So first thing when you talk about feature extraction is as time stamps you look at timestamps for a particular binary or for a particular file. So mostly all you Windows binaries have time stamps and which actually carry a time information which is a very important piece of information. Why is it important? So with time stamps that you have you can get you know the binary was compiled then the binary was created. It could be that's fine we've compiled right. And it could be compiled in say 2008. So now you know that this threat, this malware, this piece of sort of malware that is sitting on your computer is from 2008 that that kind of helps you identify and is related to a group of those malicious doctors that you're part of at that particular time. Right.

And that is why timestamps are very important and so normally attackers don't change the time. You can easily change the time stamp also. But a lot of times it gets copied over from here and there. So they don't pay that much attention to the time stamp. Right. But with you being a security expert and the intelligence threat researcher you need to look at the time stamp and always remember it and the specific features which are part of the time stamp. This is like you know a static part of it as I said and you have to basically grab these malwares without running or executing it. That's why we call it static. You know also there are other things which you need to know when you look at a timestamp.

I said you know you can identify Of course the time period how long it's been there but also what the different gangs are, what different affiliation or association it could be running to and what belongs to. Right. So one more thing as you know and a researcher you should know and it's a good thing to know is what is hot. How do you specify when you see a binary? How do you specify the time stamps for the aid and extraction part? How do you make sure you're doing it safely? Right. So that is one thing that you need to understand and you have to learn to see if techniques are around it. And this is something which again you will come.

You will get introduced in the next Book also. But that is something that you'll come to know by experience also because every malware has to be dealt differently. All right. So next is your digital certificates. Distance advocates are also another important thing. A lot of attackers use digital certificates to bypass like in your basic rules and in some companies the digital certificates help you Of course validate that oh well this is a very trusted company and so it's so difficult for Microsoft right. So now you use your scanner to see it and say hey this is digital it's this software is digitally signed by Microsoft because it has a digital certificate.

But Microsoft has not signed that both those binary files you know and if they have then there's a trust. If they have not then it is. It is because they're using a malicious name. But then the sort of kid could be old it could be something you know which has done a self-signed certificate there. So all of those things have to be dealt with and cared for. And users always trust boundaries which are from a company you can be verified by even analyzing original certificates for those drivers. So using it we know that the sources trusted are legitimate and there are other ways to go around it. Right.

So how do bad guys do it, commonly referred to as malware authors. They also use digital certificates that just mention they steal them and create them themselves. They also defecate. You know they try to do each and every wrong thing when it comes down to certificates and mind you certificates can be created on any information server but by simply generating self-signed certificates right. And then you can name it Microsoft Google whatever you want to know. But then once you look closer into the certificate it will fail. But then a lot of the malicious authors take on these techniques right.

Features Extraction Part 2

So all these tricks. Believe it or not they are very successful. They fooled a lot of bigger companies with bigger softwares out there or even most of the software they don't detect when it comes to these tactics of offering digital certificates and wrongly signed malware. All right, the next one is EXIF data. So what is acceptable, that is basically is all about your metadata from different files and it can be your exact executive bills you can use or deal else it could be any final word PDAF or different files and all of them carry some kind of metadata. So what does matter is data. Most of you should know it is basically that granular data which tells you a bit more about the file authors better data that helps you give some more information but it was created and saved by different properties you know.

So those are part of the metadata you know and it can also help in your RDF explaining the use of names actually. So another good example here is the use of language. So in a lot of the cases we overlook that. Right. So what does language have to do with malware? I mean if it's written in English or English UK versus English what does it matter if they're in Russian and Chinese got your attention. Right. So if it's Russian Chinese we can see where the originator was. And the same way you can go into different images or documents and get those features to extract where the malicious malware is coming from what language is associated with the different MIME types or even like you know if there are if there's a message or click message or something.

So to tell you all the different missions and that will help you start profiling your malicious samples. That's what we're trying to do as Trojan diligence research. Right. Always remember that we're trying to profile as deep you profile the better hunting techniques we use the better you are when it comes to succeeding with your end result. And that is finding and getting the culprits out. OK. So next let's talk about importing hash tables. So let me first explain a little bit about how this works. You should be aware that every single easy executable has an import table associated with it.

So what is an import table though. It is at a very high level. It is basically all the different deals which are used inside that binary and those are all listed together. And these all are they have their own. How many are dead, what all details what specific order they are in. So all of that basically is part of import for import hash table and this import hash table is unique for each vinery and it doesn't change because the files are always the same and Luli changes if you have changed those files the order or are written some extra code and recompiled. So I would say it's not kind of a silver bullet or anything like that but it is a good technique and. Import tables are.

You should understand what they are. Simple table hash. And then you should not read it or not really should know how to analyze it. And in the next Book I'll tell you a bit more and so you have a good grasp and understanding about the impasse which is also import table hash. All right. Another thing is your. SS DEEP now. SS DEEP is a concept which is also known as your fuzzy hash. It is basically when you're able to extract sequences of bytes in the same order from the binary. And this also specifies sequences of bytes are going to be used in that binary and the order is detected in the sample order. That can be similar to that as a set. So this is deep.

You have to look at the boundary very closely and there are other things you know which can be extracted features which would also clarify or classify a binary as in this case also. So move forward you have strings which is also another thing which helps you classify your order of how you do your feature extraction. So basically you have to get simple human readable strings from binaries or any document that those strings are sometimes you can read them from, maybe from your command and control center or another of the IP which the command and control center is using radar to see and see.

So all of those are malicious servers from the attackers so you sometimes you know like they can also have a mutex some protocol and so a mutex is also specific name assigned by a malware author to a binary so that they can avoid detection from and from the then they're part of the infected machines. And this is what you need to know from strings. What are you trying to read? You're trying to read the control and control and command center IPs of the mutex. You can also have a pretty good idea like you know what is happening and do continuous analysis and find more evidence of the different things which have been performed there. So the PDB and custom control messages are also two other things that you shouldn't know when it comes on too strong.

So the report is basically the parts which are a file or directory part when you're compiling a binary. It could be for example the PDP part. A good example would be to say I compiled a binary to be in a Windows machine and say See Seacole in Bali there's a username slash software in the visual studio or something slash you know project and file. So now from this PDP bot I can if I read it correctly to the strings I can basically identify that OK the user name could be Bolly or any other user name which is given. So there is a lot of intelligence which you can extract from there.

And Of course you know if there are any custom messages which are embedded inside the code inside the attackers basically like you know some error messages which come up and what language they are and that's it's important you know. So all these things they help you basically get a good idea about the different parts of your malware. And these are actually part of feature extraction. Right, it's pretty interesting. I hope you're enjoying the same me as I am right. So in the next class we'll be talking about another part of feature extraction and that is behaviorists behaved extraction. All right. So stay tuned and I'll see you in the next class.

Behavior Extraction Part 1

Everybody welcome back. So this is the cyber threat intelligence Book and we have covered a few of its features like extraction hunting. Now we're going to talk about behavioral extraction. So this is a dynamic way of collecting information. All right. So let's dive in. As you can see in this particular chapter there this is the third particular technique which I would say which you would need as threat intelligence researcher to go in and get evidence for a particular malware or if you have detected that particular cyber attack or if you are being tasked to to contain and to do research on something which your team is working on. All right. So far you have now learned about hunting. Right. And we've gone to different samples.

We're also extracting features statically right the static feature extraction which we did. And these two are definitely helping nuclear or classification. And you know also they hope in a specific grouping of behaviors and so forth. Right. So now we also want to see how we can segregate these groups further. And that's where these techniques which are teaching you basically take your basic understanding of a particular malware. You kind of know first you see you do your hunting phase you first see what strain of malware is that right. The next comes you start classifying that into different groups categories and sometimes these could be based on static properties also. Right.

Like the language from where they originated or originator was and so forth. And then after that you look at other specific classifications like a clustering of them and then segregation back right. All right. So now what is the main goal of beard extraction? So first let's look into that. So mainly beer extraction helps you identify unique dynamic features in a set of binary or in a binary. And this in turn helps you to classify them into specific malicious groups. This is just mind you and we're still trying to identify trying to better categorize better segregate better analyze our malware. Right. And so rock extraction works on the dynamic aspect of it. So that is the main goal behind behavior extraction. All right. OK.

So now what are the different ways in which you can see or which you need to know when working with behavior extraction are different features I would say of behavior extraction which you should be familiar with. Right. To start with beaute extractions, the first feature to be known as normal detection happens like you know how to, how do you normally detect and when does it happen. Right. And this non-medication can happen by running it and running a sample in a sandbox environment. But it is like a contained environment where you really can learn about certain behavioral properties of malware. Right. And also to all the malicious software you know how are you kind of if you know you set up your sandbox in such a way that it does not penetrate within your network.

Right. And you basically see how these features and how you can extract those features especially in the software as in the malicious software is getting implemented right. So as a threat intelligence researcher you don't need to know reverse engineering for that matter. Basically you just need to know all those different techniques to gather information in order to better a cluster cluster or better group them. Right. And once you can make these clusters you can know you can understand different behaviors also. Right. But if you have access to reverse engineering and so at some time and you are a terror threat intelligence researcher you think that you know you do need to help buffer reverser or reverse engineer you go for it and you know and take their help.

But mostly I was told that you will not need it if you are properly ordering and clustering your malware. Right. And so you can also get behavior's not only by running a sample because normally a sandbox is going to tell you if it detects an external API. Right. So when you run a sample in your sandbox environment you see all these calls going all over the network right. So the OK EPA call got made and what part of the API has been called and Viride is calling the API. And is this a different box of malware being used? Things of that sort. So you come to know all of these features you come to know and I'll discuss these in the coming classes also a little bit more in detail but this gives you a good understanding of how running a sample in the sandbox can help you. Right.

OK. So another one or another way of extraction is basically looking at your memory dumps and these are system memory dumps. This malicious piece of software is being executed right. Mostly what happens is the malware will decrypt in memory only. So that means it all. So if you look at you. If you start looking at the memory dumps you then you get to know about the certain qualities of a malware. Right. For example the red rocks you know the the remote administrator tools they have a very common feature you know and they have a configuration file which Howard normally gets decoupled in the memory right. And if you can dump that memory right and you can easily then detect what specific strain or or type of rock this is right or more remote. Mr. Tools are right. So that's really common because rats are used to administer and interact with you know a back door and whenever that is implemented or open. Right. Which is pretty pretty common I would say.

Behavior Extraction Part 2

So vivid extraction as we know it can happen how venues are in capturing malicious events and strain. So I walked you through malware in the sandbox for example. There are other malicious ways or events that get fired, not just in that particular sandbox environment. These events folders can be classified into specific families you know. And these are like behavioral families right. Furthermore if the malware is creating a file in a suspicious location like Laura Müller's malware when you first execute them they'll start replicating or creating files you know a dollar a day will they will you know take a particular or download something you know and then then drop it somewhere.

And these kinds of saws I was offered classified matters are classified as droppers so dropper is just going to drop a binary into her onto the disk. And that's what it does and then it's done right. So that's one behavior then injecting into our system process is also you must have heard right. You know sometimes malware is very, you know, conniving . They like to hide behind regular processes in your system, regular trades which are part of your battlefield. You know regular processes and so they inject themselves at different stages of the process. Right. So this injection which they do you can go in and you can classify them based on that. And what direction has been made by a particular malware. Right.

Also some of them download an exhibit to see an executable file from the Internet. And that's also one common behavior and these kinds of malware which download an easy or an executable file they're called downloaders and they just go out there. They you can go and classify them but by looking at you know malicious IPs which Richard basically uses to get the binary and to run it on your system and it's also one one thing that that can that they can do most I would say gracefully that is basically downloading it and then all these malicious IP addresses how do you classify that OK that this downloader is going to do this. This particular IP address.

So you remember if the attack floor is there there are different phases of it. Right. And you ought to see if you can segregate that dark flow. And if you can catch these different items there. The other thing is also every keystroke to enter key interception. So when you go in and basically look you've seen like you must have heard also there's always malware which can capture your keystrokes right. So these keystrokes basically there's some kind of trojans which basically kind of do this job very well. And these Trojans are mostly banking Trojans right. And I would say it's very common for banking Corydon.

So their main goal is to steal information of whatever you're typing on the keyboard and that is what their main purpose is basically to capture every keystroke that you make every you know for like basically if you're entering the account information if you're entering sensitive password information. So they just capture all that right. So other things that you shouldn't know are your A.M. and time debugging checks. Also your malware which will check if it is not being debugged or analyzed by our researcher and then you can get all the features also. Right. So a delay technique is also a very common technique.

So a lot of times you know whenever there's malware written. Right. Which has come on in command and control which has a rock base or something similar. Basically malware is going to say that I'm going to probably go and check if I'm being run in a sandbox environment right and then it has a built-in failsafe for the malware Of course. It just goes on like it or does not perform any activity and just goes silent when it finds that it is contained in my mind and it has these certain checks. A lot of the malwares have evolved right. And Of course matters that are being written by programmers you know hackers the black hackers they're smart guys right. So they know the parameters of how our sandbox works.

And then malware is basically going to sniff that if there is a if I'm being run in a particular contained environment or in a sandbox environment. So they don't execute and they put a wait time or inside it so they will wait and vote. These sleep times are to sleep cause you know they are part of all sandboxes and then what happens is that if sandbox does not see any activity it saves that well this is benign and this is not you know malicious So forget about it. And then once the sandbox containment is there, the matter is not running in a contained environment then it starts executing itself.

Behavior Extraction Part 3

So another thing is persistence. So how the malware will stay in the system after it's been rebooted. Right. Normally it's through your registry keys it tries to give these markers somewhere for it to like to for it to refire whenever you know the system comes back up. Comolli adding itself to the services also is one common thing I've noticed a lot. And also adding it to the scheduled tasks which are part of your system. Right. So this system has these recurring scheduled tasks and like insert itself as a task as a mallet. And then whenever the system reboots back up because someone's common reaction to you finding something bad on your system is like plugging it out. You know, dig it out from the network and so forth plug it off.

So these kind of there are some failsafes already built for matter has executed successful lead has already done that. It's a matter of just re-entry, maybe it's injecting itself to you. So say is your scheduled task and basically it adds persistence to the malware and then it can you know keep on coming back again and again and again. And this is also a feature that you would want to categorize or to classify for a particular behavior for a particular malware. Right. So that we as a researcher know that OK this malware behavior is that it is going in there. It is basically scheduling. It always goes in and schedules a new task or attaches itself to an already scheduled system task or something like that. Right. OK.

Now I'll go a little bit more into the events of malicious malicious software. So these are the malicious events which usually you should know about. If you look at the chaptershow versus the desktop locked and there's multiple files. Right. And then you have dumping hashes so what are these that we just walk through them quickly. So desktop lock it's really common when it comes to ransomware. R R R R so people as you know did what they do is they do a ransom lock. And this is basically they lock your desktop and then you pay them something. And this is often known as ransom lock.

We know that we hear the news a lot these days that hey a whole company will shut down their desktops are locked and somebody is demanding. And they are. They are part of a tie which is a ransom better attack but this attack is also called ransom law. Right. But everything is locked down until they pay something in bitcoins currency or whatever the transaction is. But we have different classes you know which tell you and prepare your staff at different levels on how to react to ransomware to phishing attacks and so forth. I would say like it or you go look at it but they don't cover that in this Book. All right. So next is malicious events. You should know like multiple files basically all right each other right.

So this might be like a file infector that normally is going to scan your whole system and then override your system binaries or any other documents in your documents folder that have some malicious code and basically body itself somehow some variant of it starts overwriting. So it does multiple file overwriting right. And this is called the file infector for the binary. And another one is dumping hashes. So dumping ashes from memory is interesting and it's a malicious event for sure. There might be a malicious event that is just trying to get you to your say or the Sam database and Sandy debater's if you don't know it is then all the debates and windows which holds all your credentials and so forth you know you like a username password is unknown.

So dumping ashes from memory uses that technique to go in and infect your system. All right. So next I think of it because you talked about a different strategy. Also about passive DNS passive DNS What does that mean get you familiar with that subclass of DNS. I'm going to go and give you a bit more details in the different Books also but I know there are some examples which I would want you to also get familiar with. Right. But just for the sake of this class and I'm just giving you an overview, let's say that you know you have your DNS pointing to a specific IP address right. And so you know that OK if I enter this domain name the DNS server will serve up as being searched from this IP address. Right.

So passive DNS or the DNS D-B queries are used in your passive passive DNS straight and it's always queering by or DNS DB. Right. And that gets that passive value. So you can go in. You can basically go in your Deena's D.B and you can know the history of readiness and what the different IP addresses are. This particular D DNS has been associated with over a period of time. And this helps you to build out a proper crime scene or map out the malicious domain name or to confirm if this is a malicious website or not. Also in the opposite side you can come to know what IP has been pointing toward DNS names so you can see what domains and different IPs have mapped or changed over a period of time.

It is good to keep this history and the NAACP does a good job for this. Right. OK. All right so now you have come to the end of class for that is a beer or extraction. I hope you had as much fun as I did. I think these techniques are really really cool and really nice you know as a researcher and further on you know when you're classifying your malicious software you know software richer and richer or researching on you can use these techniques in your work environment or as a consultant. All right, thank you for joining. And next we'll be talking about clustering and the correlation technique.

Clustering and Correlation

I Welcome back. We've gone through different phases and this and this class and what we're going or clustering and correlation we and cyber threat intelligence phases or Of course and and again we already went through behavior behavioral integration in the last one. OK. So all the different techniques which I'm talking to you about are very I would say crucial when you are trying to extract information. So we started with different levels. Right we started with getting to know your malware then identifying it and knowing the different features offered. Then understanding the behavior of it. Right, so what is the behavior?

Now in this class we're going to talk about the different clustering and correlation of your malware, how you further divide it cluster into clusters and so forth. Right. So to start with let's look at the main goal behind clustering and correlation right. So clustering in coalition is basically used to classify malware based on its different features and its different behaviors. And what we do and basically what we do is we classify it and then extract it and correlate the information to either the already existing data or our own research and understand attack flow off of that particular malware. Right.

So it is a technique to understand the full picture of the attack flow and attack vector and different dockworkers which that particular malware word would have. Right. So let's understand clustering and correlational but more right a little bit more details around it. So basically clustering is referred to as nodes right and nodes are specific objects that have a specific feature set and a specific behavior. So you have a node which has got a specific feature set and a specific behavior and that is how the node is basically classified. So collectively those are different objects because when they're created then clusters are formed. Which bit really has different features associated with it. Right.

Some of the common features of all clustering nodes are timestamped; you have an impasse. SS DEEP in visual certifications all of these different features and they are part of your particular node and how a node cluster is being classified. Right. Many of them are static features. Right. And they can help us basically classify a particular malware and they're really, you know, important and very vital to you as a trained intelligence researcher also. All right. So another thing we have to do. They are clustering nodes you have properties right. And all of the behaviors that we detected earlier as you remember like you know your keylogger or download or drop or you're talking more than in earlier classes also. So those are the properties for a specific node but this will help us also as I said to segregate based on these behavioral properties if you did in the earlier class so now you know OK what are the different properties.

So this helps you segregate basically into different groups. So we have all these different node groups which basically have their own specific features and behaviors. Right. But also if we say it's a downloader or a backdoor that can also help us add more context into a specific group or even further classify it into its own micro clusters or something like that. All right. So this gives a good understanding of how properties are, how important they are, how important they are and how clustering nodes is and how they kind of flow when it comes to malware. Right. Next is basically correlation. So how. So once you have information we need to exploit it like how do you get that like. And can this be done by using different techniques right?

So a lot of the time coalition is done using gravity being right. Basically you want a rough draft if you don't know it is like a relational database but it's based on your sequel. And it lets you basically connect all the dots and it has a structure or a design but not relational like you see in your traditional RDBMS. So gravity is not a sequel database. Right. And it is just nothing but a collection of nodes and edges. Right. If you're familiar with no terminologies, that's what it is. Symptoms collections also are used. So let me show you basically how graphics I look at this picture right here in the chapter. It's basically said it is just a connection between your nodes and relationships and properties right.

To do that at a very high level. That's how I know it is that there are no defined relationship relationships that have properties associated with it. So all of these different things that we have that we just found out using our behavioral phase and other hunting phases and all. So all of them they get classified under these they know that these relationships are defined within the nodes and then properties that are associated with these different relationships and graphs they said is a very cool way to interconnect all these. As a researcher you should know that. And then after we can store all this information very neatly and very secret like you know separation is there and segregation is also built inside you know no database. All right. Another example here.

If you see on the chart it is basically from counter-strike. So this is documented behavior for the real organization of crime which took place. And this crime was carried out on an organization as I said. So also you pay some special attention to the different parts of the graphic the Howard is structured and you can understand that the head researcher lead is based around the correlation but that is the final goal of it right. So a quick glance you can see in the middle of this image there is a specific identifier. So this identifier basically helps you further analyze the other portions like how you can know these are these hexadecimal values and stuff from which you learn that OK.

Now this is the divide and then you can see if anything else is said that there's a fire. So when analyzing specific behaviors you can get a specific key and then if you drop that into a particular software program system or something then you can connect that to other information like IP addresses and then you understand the bigger scheme of things the bigger picture that where the origination is happening what strain is this. Right. So it all starts from one identifier. And further you can go and dig into it and solve real real crime. I would say. All right. So this actually concludes our class on clustering and correlation and a lot of interesting things. He went over and again tried to look at the diagram again and try to see what you can make out of that. Right. All right. Thanks for joining. I'll see you next class.

Threat Actor Attribution Part 1

So you are in the cyber threat intelligence phases or view Of course. And this is the different phases and when it comes down to intelligence and this one is around threat or retribution. All right. So if you look at this chart we have covered close to the fifth one and we've covered like a hunting feature extraction extraction flustering. Right. So now you have your features you have taken out the behaviors you have clustered there you've seen the properties of the nodes you have classified them. So the idea of like you know all the information which you need. Right. But the big question still remains who is behind this attack. How is that person you know that trained actor right? So who is behind that attack? And that's what you want to know. The threat actor attributed how she identified that.

Right. So here what we do is you would have to locate the doctor behind the malicious cluster of them to find. So for example you need to answer these questions like you know where they are located. Now the one person team grows up into a gang . You know what you want to classify it as. Right so that is what this particular trait of actor Bhushan as the terrorist threat intelligence researcher I would highly recommend you to understand because you have to see you know you have the center standing or to verify that's her doctor's right. And this will we hope you do with that. All right so now let's look at the goal as we do in all of them. So the main goal for Dr.

retribution is to get the doctor behind the malicious clustered and define. So for example you need to answer these questions like you know you are you know the very very it was originated from and it is located. All these will be answered right. So as I said as a researcher you need to be ready with this answer right. And the question for us begins as vaid they are located. Which continent? Which country they are located in is the next important attribute you wouldn't need to be aware of who is sponsoring them. Usually you'll be surprised 99 percent of the time they're sponsored. Sometimes an attack can be sponsored, say by a nation-straight nation state. For example, it could be you know Russian Gorme and are like the Chinese government or any other garment sponsoring them. Now they are a malicious attack. Then we see there's a lot of these in the U.S.

you read in your newspapers in 2016 are full with that 20:17 already talks are going on that you know a lot of you know nation state sponsored attacks are being carried out you know. So the Chinese Gurman like it could be like now. So any government in the Nigerian army could be anything you know so that we know there are a lot of these attacks which are being done and similar attacks are known to be launched by us also. So USA also sponsors a lot of these attacks and this is as I had mentioned before also it is cyber war going on right. And this is the next level of warfare and you don't even need to find a single bullet. You can still take down a whole country so what sector and industry are these people targeting. Normally.

The groups are going to focus on a specific sector. Right. There's always a reason or a goal behind a particular attack when it gets launched and is always always aimed at a particular sector. It could be the financial institutions that are banks or probably they are just trying to focus on say a nuclear plant taking your brand off line you know or are trying to damage the nuclear plant. I just saw it happen last 2016 in that air and also help you to categorize who these doctors are. So this will give you good information. When you see what industry what sector if they're focusing on. Right. And there's a sea of infrastructure right. The command and control infrastructure.

Those who are new as I said combined command and control sojourned are known as CNC command controllers that where they are located and this is from this is where it wants to get access to a particular system or to a particular network. This is from where they launch the commanders where the information goes to or from where they were ; they'd like either a remote desktop or terminal server and get into the different ports to learn what the different ports are open. Now what is the operating system they are running?

Are those details you know around them you know and so these kinds of you to help us understand the C-2 infrastructure also in some cases because you can not get. You cannot backtrack them because they always you know wipe out their tracks but then the kind of behaviors which they launch are the kind of things to do in my mind or in their command and control see to infrastructure. This is how you specify that.

Threat Actor Attribution Part 2

The thing is your tactics techniques and procedures that you should know also the tactics techniques and procedures are commonly referred to as a TBS. All right. So TTP is certainly a due diligence researcher. You will always be dealing with DGP which means how they get into the system. What are the tactics, techniques and procedures for getting into were infiltrating into a system. Right. So the techniques being used here are mostly what the bad guys do as they have different procedures and different skill sets which they use and which is basically to help you identify and define a specific group.

Right. And here probably you might need somebody like a reverse or a reverse engineer which can also help you identify the different tactics and techniques that a particular bad guy or a hacker is using and that you are looking at. Right. What a different algorithm than the corruption algorithms they're using right now. How are they decoding the boundaries and what are they really decoding in the memory. For example is the malicious code called induction happening it isn't the memory or it's coming from the result of a binary. All that detail you know you can get right. And also another thing is how you get persistence into a system.

And I mentioned that earlier also you can get persistence free registry keys. You can launch some you know system tasks you can do services COM object there different techniques you know in which you can basically gain persistence right. So these techniques you know are those with the help of a reverse engineer you can also they can also help you to understand these traits and better basically. All right. So the other thing is that you know when you're being initially compromised how do these bad guys get into the system can they. Did they get into a spate phishing attack or can it be just through a Facebook link which is shared and for you to download the malware right.

You just thought oh this is a message from a friend or from a group or something and he just clicked on it and now boom is now Mowery been downloaded. So all these are different. You know spear fishing techniques are social and techniques that basically also define that specific group of doctors. Also privilege privilege escalation. So when there's an escalation in privileges This is basically even when somebody has entered your network and they are trying different techniques in order to try to escalate privileges of use or make it a sysadmin and so forth. Right. And either use sudo or some other accounts right to some of some others.

Our persistence and lateral movements are there. How precise positions there are and if they're moving laterally within the network to penetrate deep or not very important is how they spread inside the network. So different groups use different techniques and it is very important to define and specify those groups. So once you spend more time doing this classification and reading you know the behavior of the entry points, how they're entering into a particular network, how they're hiding themselves, how they're building persistence, how they're even moving inside, how they're doing the escalation. You will slowly slowly try to understand and get in the shoes of the hacker as an intelligence researcher.

Now things will start becoming fun to you because now you know that this is how the bad guys think. This is the behavior that you do and all this default to this group. In that group it could be hundreds of them but then you know exactly the trend which group it is because you have identified them, you've segregated classified flustered, you're putting in the right words giving them the right properties. Right. So last one hundred go is the exfiltration strategy. So how do they steal the information? Right. And that's the very important thing. Everybody has their own technique right. They upload some files. It's why they're using specific protocol requests or either it's VI or raw socket.

Even they use certain proxies in a certain way in different countries. So how are they doing this? Right. What information they are extracting and what is the format of the information which has been extracted. So this is all part of their exfiltration strategy. Right. And all this helps you understand the proper misleader property and helps you classify and identify and catalog this behavior of a particular malicious group or a particular malicious or Dr.. So it's important to note the key taken away. And I will say from this from just these last few chapters is if not a true doctor can be identified the whole threat intelligence effort is useless.

That's what I say. And at the end of the day you can fire your phone. The malware can do your feature you can do behavior you can do clustering but if you don't know who is behind their attack you cannot dig down that organized crime or that organized crime branch. All right. Thanks for joining us and I'll see you in the next class and we're talking about another aspect that is tracking.

Tracking

Welcome back to cyber certain intelligence phases or your Book we are going to talk about tracking . So now as a threat intelligence researcher you have gone and you have gone in and done the hunting you've gone in and done the feature collection you've done behavioral organization you've done no classification. So now there's more to do because now you also identify the doctor right. So the goal is that a set is to anticipate new attacks and identify new variants proactively. Right. And that is one of the main things which we will talk about in this class. So what is the goal of tracking the goal is to anticipate new attacks and identify new variants proactively. So next let me tell you how you can understand and meet this goal right. Because you have to understand it and how you would do it proactively. Right.

So we have always been talking about different mindsets and disBook also. All right. So in track and tracking itself I want you to get familiar with certain techniques. All right the first one is DNS passive DNS actually. So what happens is that attackers can switch from a new domain or point to a domain that has the new IP address. All this can be mined out by creating the passive DNS database. So by creating this you simply For example if somebody has pointed their domain to a new IP or they are too frequently changing to new IPs so you can get all that data from passive Deena's database. All right. Another technique is Internet port scan. So that's a risky but very interesting approach.

So basically if you know that your seat to the command and control is listening into a specific port ordered or different ports you can go and scan the Internet and find those two infrastructures. So basically you're going up a little bit, you're going into their world. You do expose something and that's why I said it's a little risky. Right. So next up is lookups. So you have the features, you have the behavior you can create, you are rude or even Sinatra will still try and hunt through all this to buy the store or go into your own database in your company with hundreds and thousands of samples and try to search for those features. So basically it's basically look up sites or virus software that has a nice lookup engine and so users use VirusTotal.

So as you can put in your Yatta rules saying that you know that they're matching a particular string, a particular API byte, anything email address. And once you put in your yard rules you can also tell in VirusTotal that hey whenever a match is you do find a match. You basically send me an email so I know I get the no phone right. Or the thing that you should be familiar with is your impact. Ss d SS DEEP hash is a very important word also. As you remember, impassionate hash properties are also there. They also help in defining some that is between samples and then you can use it to further track and find those or some other sample just similar to that.

Right next is your open source intelligence that is called or isn't and so with this information. This is all open source available on your search engine and stuff. You can go and check for IP addresses of all the code off to say the command

and control center and also probably you can find the email addresses associated with your new domains created with different sets of information. Right. So that is the power of open source intelligence. Again I don't recommend this one that is the gang infiltration into hacking forums. Obviously you can keep tracking them and still still like in the hacking forums. They were disgusted with a lot of stuff. The new releases of the tool and so forth. So if you're reading them you can get all this information.

And I would highly recommend that you strictly just observe, don't participate and don't go too much deep into it, don't commit anything you know to these forums or hacking or gang infiltrations right. But this normally is done with the help of some law and order like the FBI. And also they have some secret agents out and there's you you don't know who you're talking to and who you want to just act as if you are a hacker and now on the other side is Asia and you could go to jail also just to let you know so be very careful. All right. All right. So this concludes our tracking class and the last step we're going to discuss in the next class that is taking down.

Again keep things in mind. Don't go overboard when you're looking into when you're trying to know the track or trying to get into some certain you know malicious software or always a member or born as a church researcher. All right. And keep law enforcement on your side. Well thanks for joining and I'll explain more in the hour takedown class and how you get the bad guys, how you track them down and track them but how do you get them to jail or to dismantle that operation. Thank you.

Conclusion

My buddy will come back. This is the cyber threat intelligence certification and we are talking about different phases. There will be phases. This is the last phase and this phase is called Taking down. All right. So taking down is a critical technique for you all to understand and this is also a final step. So far you understood everything about the group about you know you know like you know what the ATP group says. So there is a group called Our network or cyber. All right. So you'd give a name to that corrupted group Pollards always has identification as a researcher you are also tracking them and probably it's time for you to take them down.

So in order to take down a group it has to be a joint effort between your team and the local law enforcement. Mind you again the local law enforcement. So if you are trying to take down a group which is not in the legal jurisdictions of your country you have to work with local law and local law enforcement. Usually like in some law enforcement bodies which are very common. Europol Interpol the FBI depends on the country. Right. But you should always work with them and it has to be really joint and a fully functional collaborative effort. All right. So first let's look at the goal right there and say the goal here is to fully dismantle organized crime operations. Your training goal is as a researcher you want to first do something.

You've done your work, you've done the research you're identified, now you want to dismantle them so they can or do further no harm to your organization, to your client or to any other similar organization. Right. So taking down the bad guys basically physically getting them arrested or stopping their operation. Right. So what are some of the different techniques when it comes down to taking them down? So let me get you familiar with that first right. So one of the really cool ones and one which I like is called sinkhole. So cynical as we're going to talk about that in detail at a very high level. This technique basically involves you taking over the C-2 infrastructure and the command and control infrastructure by using different approaches that we're going to go over that we went to earlier also.

So and then what you do is that everything all the different hosts the infection but then infected hosts are all going or going to all point to you know. Right. And they're not even a point to the bad guys and the traffic is not directed to your server so you kind of intercepted and now you are kind of behaving as if as a single you're taking over the seat to infrastructure. Right. And what this does is this approach is that you get are you going to also do a little detail on it. But at the end of the day your simple goal is just stopping the operation. That is what you are.

You are focusing on the right. Also you can do like a man in the middle attack which basically means that that was all forward all the traffic to my box and then forwarded to the bad guy. So you're kind of siphoning off kind of checking everything it's going to siphon through you basically. Right.

And so this is the mad man in the middle. So you think it's a bad guy. That they are still operating. So David and you are monitoring what they're operating on and what information they're going back and forth on the pipe and you are in there and you're monitoring everything and all the actions. Right.

And from a single point and we don't let the victims get reinfected that's also one thing to stop anything which is to which is a red flag to us. Right. All right. Another thing is another tracking technique you should know as hacking forums or hacking forums is a very common way to take them down. And there for example there was a hacking for cold or dark cold right. You must have heard of that cold case. If not then it was basically hacking from a specific phone which was very famous for selling and discussing exploits or exploits for operating systems and so forth. And that was the dark gold confirms right.

So it was taken down. And one of the most common law enforcement things that they want to do is to shut it down and shut it down to take the owners and and the take down. Basically what happens is as I said always in takedowns you need to have full support and collaboration right. I feel like the country law enforcement has to be velká collaborated Countrywide or our continent wide or nationwide effort. Right. Let's say if there is an IP protected which has been attacked from China it's not easy to ask China. Hey guys the group is going to this Internet service provider ISP which is hosting this IPN. And dig this down please. That's not going to happen. Same as with other Russia there.

The USA is also launching similar attacks too. So there are some things that you should know other researchers will not happen so don't try to go that route. Maybe you will dig a hole for yourself. So finally let's talk about the summary of this class. We have gone through all the different techniques and you understood how taking down works also. So we started with different phases of torch intelligence efforts which side and which kind of event or event were like the big picture. There are some cool techniques and skills we talked about. And finally the goal of that is basically tracking down and taking down the doctors. Right. Vyle we're doing this. We also totally like that you know behaviors are very important.

Basically segregation is really important. And also then consolidating all of that into two nodes using graph B. So all of these different techniques. Right. And in the end everything leads down to if you can't be fully accessible and if they are a jurisdiction which you know the FBI Interpol Europol has and can get you in and stop that effort then God is basically going in there and stopping the bad guys right. Usually some of the bad guys also operate from different IP addresses and different servers. But once of you if the good part is if you if you know the physical address and if you know which country they're originating from and if

You've done your research in a very wealthy man I would say Fastrak well-mounted fashion. Now you know the address, you know the IP addresses, you know there's two ways you know which do different and different types of espies they're coming from. So you've gone and looked into their Siku infrastructure. You've also gone in and filtered their traffic through your particular infrastructure. So now the bad guys you know where they are you can take them down. And this is a collaborative effort and you can go to Interpol Europol local FBI local law enforcement. All right. So hope you enjoyed this disBook about trade intelligence and thanks for joining. I will see you in the next Book and get into more details on all these different techniques.

Don't miss out!

Visit the website below and you can sign up to receive emails whenever SADANAND PUJARI publishes a new book. There's no charge and no obligation.

https://books2read.com/r/B-A-YJFBB-XSUZC

BOOKS 2 READ

Connecting independent readers to independent writers.

Also by SADANAND PUJARI

Master The Psychology Of Weight Loss Via Hypnosis Build Healthy Sleep Habits Learn The Art Of Meditation Improve People Management And Build Employee Engagement
Content Marketing Masterclass Create Content That Sells Cyber Security For Normal People Protect Yourself Online Kanban Fundamentals How To Become Insanely Productive
Positive Psychology Art Therapy: Certified Training Bookkeeping In Quickbooks Online (Bookkeeping & Accounting)
Business Impact of Digital Transformation Technologies Learn How to Protect & Restore Yourself from Negative Energy
Generative AI - From Big Picture, To Idea, To Implementation